THE J

Dolan worked out that Markovicz was now reaching the crescendo of his performance. His eyes suddenly riveted in on Markovicz' expression, and he felt a sudden total confusion because he knew there was something deeply, inexplicably wrong. He turned quickly to Julie, to check her reaction. Nothing. Her eyes moving slightly, as the string of green balls tumbled around the controlled ellipse. He quickly looked back, confirmed he'd been right. Markovicz was trying to hide it, suppress it in grim, stretched muscles across his face. But he couldn't do anything with the look in his eyes. The look he couldn't hide was terror.

The Juggler

IAN KENNEDY MARTIN

SPHERE BOOKS LIMITED

First published in Great Britain by
William Heinemann Ltd, 1985

Published by Sphere Books Ltd, 1986
27 Wrights Lane, London W8 5TZ
Reprinted 1986

TRADE
MARK

Set in 10 on 11½pt Linotron Melior

Printed and bound in Great Britain by
Cox & Wyman Ltd, Reading

The day of the juggler started late. Dolan awoke in a motel room that smelled of scotch whisky. He felt flushed and a lot iller than with his usual hangover. There was a minute of disorientation, then he realized the room smell came from him, had originated in the empty bottle by the bed, and the closed windows. It was Napa in an August heatwave. He looked at his watch, realized with a start that two appointments were wrecked, and groaned. He pulled himself out of bed. It was a week to his twenty-seventh birthday. He felt eighty-five.

The shower cubicle was too small. The thermostat was stuck ten degrees too hot. The bath towel was the size of a hand towel. He realized it was going to be one of those days. He made the shower short, dressed quickly and staggered out into the boiling sun.

He drove south past possible breakfast places. As he started to steer the hire car into one forecourt his stomach turned over, as a warning not to touch. He drove on. He would get coffee at Julie's.

His ex-wife lived in the southern beginnings of the town, in a clapboard two-up-two-down near the junction where the Old Sonoma Road met Highway 29. She was waiting for him. She had the same face she'd practised a year back in the divorce hearing about alimony.

'You're an hour late. Where were you?'

The question was rhetorical. 'Overslept. I need a coffee.'

'At the professor's.'

He didn't have the reserve to argue. Anyhow she sat into the car, and she wasn't going to move. He did a U- turn and headed back the way he'd come. It was interesting to him that by her silence alone she was able to convey several messages, like, 'Don't speak to me,' and 'You look like shit,' and 'You're always late, always let me down,' and 'Jesus, are you still drunk?'

The professor had rented a weekend home with a rear garden that looked like a city dump. It sat alone surrounded by abandoned lots, a half-mile northeast of where the nineteenth-century architecture section of the town finally ran out. It was near the Tulocay Cemetery on the east side of the river.

Professor Markovicz' wife Greta looked like she had a hangover too. Dolan greeted her guardedly. She came in two versions. One was the sober-suited grim-faced ex-Eastern European with the conversation pattern of an SS commander ordering hostages to be shot, the other was the drunk, when her face dissolved into red patches and her hair stood out sideways. Her outlook this morning was mid-distance between the two visions.

'I'd love some coffee?' Dolan asked as he limped towards the house. Somehow he'd slept in a cricked leg position. There was a sharp pain in the right thigh.

'We run out of coffee. I got wine open.'

The second piece of information was gratuitous – Greta Markovicz always had wine open.

Dolan thought about wine and his stomach didn't heave. 'A glass. White?'

'Château St. Jean, their nice Chardonnay,'78.'

'That's a good wine,' Dolan offered.

'I know it's a good wine. Is expensive. The

professor wish to see you, round the back.'

He set off shakily across the rubbish heap towards a rickety wooden carport. At the rear of the carport he could see a battered Jeep, and a large truck painted grey. The professor was sitting on a broken garden chair, a hammer in his hand. He'd knocked off two sides of a long wooden crate.

'Hi.'

The professor turned, studied Dolan with the first look he gave most people. It said, 'Who are you?' and then dissolved into a slight nod of recognition. 'Good afternoon. Are you late?'

'I'm late. I'm sorry.'

'I want you to look at this.' The professor pointed to the new turbine pump engine sitting in the crate. 'When you worked in a garage you ever saw one of these?'

'A pump engine?'

'Give me your opinion. What d'you think are the revolution tolerances of a turbine this size?'

He was not ready to make calculations, with a splitting head, about pump engines. He sat down heavily on the edge of the crate, and looked the turbine over. 'I don't know anything about pump turbines, but if the rev counter is red-lined at fifteen thousand, it would probably tolerate twenty thousand. But I don't know . . . you know, we don't get turbines in a repair shop.'

The professor shrugged. 'Keep a secret, John Dolan.'

'Yes?'

The old man's cold blue eyes were on the pump engine, speculating, calculating. Now he turned to Dolan. 'John, don't tell anyone you saw this . . . this piece of equipment.'

'Right, if you say so.'

'A secret?'

Dolan couldn't work out why it should be secret

that the professor had acquired a turbine engine. 'Right.'

'Now we are late.' The professor got up smartly. 'We must never keep millionaires waiting. You drive my Greta, and your Julie, and yourself. I'll drive the truck. I follow you. Don't go fast.'

'Julie can drive Greta. I'll drive the truck with you.'

'No,' the old man said sharply.

Dolan headed back for the house.

The estate of William Hill Hunt II edged along the fold of the east valley up from its better known neighbour, the Carneros Creek Winery. The Hunt winery had been established five years ago. Dolan was not looking forward to the wine-tasting at the Hunt place. He'd tried a recent Cabernet Sauvignon. His verdict had been that the cellar master should be shot. But he wanted to see the Hunt place. One of the oldest homes in Napa, now much extended. George Yount was supposed to have stayed there around 1830, the time when the famous Napa cholera broke out and cleared the valley of thousands of Indians. Indians and their bison didn't go with white men and their vines. Cholera had made Napa.

They saw the Hunt spread from two miles away, a white long silhouette of house, surrounded by low chais. The white softly counterpointing the gentle green rise of hills behind, and the grey and green patchwork of vines carpeting downhill. The hire car purred past the vineyards and the thousands of lines of young plants. These melted into a blur or appeared to slide backwards or forwards according to the speed of the car. The road as Dolan drove up to the house suddenly became full of unexpected cambers, as if the domain wished to be alien to intrusion from a century that didn't belong here in such solitude.

Julie pointed out the hidden opening among the

trees that was the stone driveway to the house. Dolan steered the car on to the wider ramp that led up to the house. He checked the rear mirror. Professor Markovicz, who had begun to tail back in the grey truck, now lumbered some more speed into the vehicle, and it was catching up.

They parked the hire car and the grey truck in a line with a dozen expensive-looking limousines in front of the house. The front double doors of the villa opened and a butler looked out. He disappeared leaving the door open. A moment later a tall man came out.

The man's beige silk suit was impeccably cut, but like the clothes of any aristocrat of commerce, it seemed there simply to hang on him. There appeared to be no overall cohesion to his body, his hands were large, his nails carefully manicured, his hair, grey with streaks of silver, was cut neatly, but disarranged. Dark, cool eyes, moving constantly, and a clear intelligence, somehow at home behind the thin patrician nose and the straight-line heavy eyebrows. He offered an outstretched hand. 'I'm William Hunt.'

The professor was the first to shake it. 'Leon Markovicz. This is Greta, my wife. And two good friends, Julie Dolan, and John Dolan.'

'And this is your truck?' The patrician head inclined towards the grey truck.

'My equipment.'

'And you're going to do some magic for us . . .?' Hunt's eyes were giving Markovicz a calculating appraisal.

'I will demonstrate what I spoke of in my correspondence.'

'I look forward to that. But first you'll meet my guests, and have lunch.' He turned to Dolan. 'I understand you're a wine correspondent?'

'*Village West.*'

'I'm sure I've read your column. I'll be interested to hear what you have to say about our wines. Please follow me.'

The house was deep and gloomy with high frieze-worked ceilings. In the hall there were tapestries, several French gilt clocks, and oil paintings – the darkness here was deep enough to make the paintings look undistinguished, though if Dolan guessed correctly, they were probably worth as much as the estate. The atmosphere of the rooms had been carefully calculated. The richness of the furnishings was to be overlaid by a sense of informal comfort. Dolan felt the planning had worked. It was a house to feel at ease in.

There were other guests – half a dozen. They were obviously from Hunt's world of high finance, with their relaxed conversation and practised exchanges. They were people who'd made their pile, and didn't give a damn for anything any more except the higher social graces. Dolan parried their looks. His, Julie's and the Markovicz' dress had a great deal more informality than the decorators had planned for the house.

The informal grouping was now mobilized into a little crocodile as a butler came in, announced lunch, and set off to lead the guests through the halls to the long dining room. Its walls were painted with murals of olden days' vineyard workers picking and pressing grapes. The lunch was leisured and episodic and designed around a sommelier ferrying in magnums of French wine. Hunt saved his own wine product for the last, when tastes were dulled and the flow of alcoholic enthusiasm heightened.

About three o'clock Hunt stood up. 'Ladies and gentleman, Professor Leon Markovicz of Davis College is going to put on a show for us. In the gardens. I think you'll be interested.'

The butler had arranged some chairs out on the side lawns. Markovicz disappeared into the long grey truck parked just out of sight of the lawns. Dolan gave up and offered an order to one of the circulating waiters for a third glass of brandy. He felt ill now, out of things, out of sympathy with the surroundings, and the other guests, the fat cats and their leisured voices and easy acceptance of each other, and exclusion of Julie, the Markovicz's and himself.

The guests eventually sat in a semicircle. Markovicz reappeared from the grey truck. He looked harassed. Then he made the decision, walked smartly up in front of the assembly. 'Ladies and gentlemen, I am your juggler. You have perhaps seen jugglers, in circus or burlesque? Some use Indian clubs. Others use doggie balls, like this.' He put his hand in his pocket and pulled out and held a small hard rubber ball. 'Heavy rubber. What your dog chews on, plays with. I will now juggle nine balls. This is probably a world record. What it should demonstrate is that here is a man who perhaps can do the impossible.'

Half his audience weren't listening. The same genial voices murmured on, just pitched a little lower.

Dolan sat there, a hint of something, a disquiet, a tiny alarm bell ringing somewhere in the back of his alcohol-bruised mind. The old professor was looking very mad, but oddly serene, unperturbed by the fact that most of his audience of Hunt's people were ignoring him. Dolan had never seen Markovicz juggling anything. It seemed such a bizarre talent to suddenly decide to demonstrate to this particular group of people.

'Have I your attention?' Markovicz asked his audience.

The conversation of the Hunt guests ceased.

Markovicz reached into his jacket pocket and picked out another ball. He started to juggle the two green balls. Then a hunch of shoulder, a sleight of hand, and he had one hand into, and out of, his right pocket, with another ball launched up into the pattern of rising and falling.

Dolan turned his head slightly, located Hunt's interested appraisal of the odd event happening. A guest, a woman, sitting next to Hunt, was whispering to him. Hunt didn't look as if he was listening.

Dolan turned back. Markovicz had executed two more quick digs into his pockets. There were now five balls arcing, yo-yoing up and down. Another hunch of shoulder, and quick movement of left hand, now dipping into pocket, and a sixth ball joined the green circumferencing of the others.

He suddenly realized he was going to be sick. The rich lunch, the surfeit of wine on top of the lonely motel hit at the scotch bottle last night, the unventilated sleep, had all come to an arrangement to evacuate his gut. He got up groggily, and headed fast back into the coolness of the house.

He found a lavatory and threw up, and immediately felt better. He headed back to the garden.

He sat down again, worked out the juggler was now reaching the crescendo of his performance. His eyes suddenly riveted in on Markovicz' expression, and he felt a sudden total confusion because he knew there was something deeply, inexplicably wrong. He turned quickly to Julie, to check her reaction. Nothing. Her eyes moving slightly, as the string of green balls tumbled around the controlled ellipse. He quickly looked back, confirmed he'd been right. Markovicz was trying to hide it, suppress it in grim, stretched muscles across his face. But he couldn't do anything with the look in his eys. The look he couldn't hide was terror.

He got up again, crossed to Julie, sat down beside her. 'What's going on here?' he whispered urgently.

'What is it?' She turned on him sharply.

'Look at his eyes.'

But the juggler had arrived at the end of the act and the expression Dolan had seen was gone.

'Nine doggie balls, ladies and gentlemen,' the professor announced, his voice hard, precise, his body still stooped forward, like a wrestler looking for an opening, his hands still a blur, chaperoning the circling chain of green. Then his palms went down and the balls hit the ground in little bounces and rolls.

There was some bemused applause. Dolan's eyes went from Markovicz to the audience. The audience was embarrassed, anxious now to offer soft comments clothed in superior smiles to each other. None of them knew what the hell it was about. Dolan spotted Mrs Markovicz sitting stone still, expressionless. Julie was leaning back in her chair, looking vague.

His eyes went to Hunt. He revised his assessment about Hunt being part of the embarrassment shared by his rich friends. Hunt's face was a mask of calculations. Some intense message was going on between him and the professor. Markovicz stock still on the lawn, the green balls at his feet.

Dolan pressed Julie again. 'What the hell was that about . . .'

She shrugged. 'God knows. Party trick. But I think he lost his audience.'

Hunt had now got up and gone over to Markovicz. He took him by the arm and led him away from the murmuring guests, out across the wide lawn and round in the direction of the front of the house.

'I'm going to be sick,' Dolan offered Julie, saw her mouth turn down in contempt as he lurched up. He paced fast again into the house.

The lavatory he'd used before was locked. He moved deeper into the house, blundered into an oak-panelled den, crossed it, spotted an open door into a white cubicle. He went in and vomited.

He washed his face and stood in front of the basin, trying to decide if he was well enough to go out again. Then he heard someone on a wall phone in the corridor. It wasn't Hunt's voice, and he wasn't even sure it was one of Hunt's guests. The voice was thick, low and angry. 'Put me through to Tower,' the voice ordered. Dolan dried his face on a soft monogrammed towel.

'Tom, I'm speaking from Hunt's. Markovicz has done it! I've seen it! It's living. Jesus. He's got a big grey truck. Don't argue with me!' The voice was rising from anger towards hysteria. 'He's done it. He's pulled it off. Jesus, he's pulled it off . . .!'

Dolan adjusted his shirt collar, walked out. There was no one there.

Six weeks later Leon Markovicz was dead. Dolan read it in the papers. The professor had gone swimming. His clothes had been found on Redondo Beach. When he read the small by-line, for some reason his mind didn't go back to images of Markovicz lecturing – he'd attended a year of the professor's lectures – or to the many evenings he and Julie had spent with Markovicz and wife. When he read the item, page five of the *L.A. Times*, his mind flashed back immediately to Hunt's place, and the two events. They were the conversation of the anonymous telephone caller in the corridor outside the oak-panelled den, and the terror in Markovicz' expression as he juggled the green balls, on the wide lawns of the winery at Napa.

He sat in the battered Chrysler, picked some gristle out of his teeth which shouldn't have been in a breakfast 'Dolores' quarter-pounder, looked at his watch, half past ten, and no Detective Hagen.

Hagen was sharp on his dates, Dolan knew that. The man had refined efficiency into every corner of his sober hours. Drunk, on a bender, a different matter. Don Hagen would sometimes disappear up the end of several magnums for a week – and then come back with some overpractised excuse – 'the old war wound.' Hagen had never been in any wars except the ones he conducted on his own on the streets of L.A. And the Police Department didn't fire him because he was fine at his wars, and good to have around the forty odd weeks of the year that he did show up. Karma is what Hagen had achieved out on the streets. Dolan had worked out that even when Hagen shot people, he would have a peaceful expression.

He angled his face to the right, into the streams of air-conditioning from the ticking motor via the fascia vent. Hot out there. The car parked semi-illegally in the forecourt of Beverly Hills police station. An image-distorting heatwave September day. Few autos moving on the alongside boulevard, clear sun bleaching out the features of the few pavement walkers. Los Angeles more or less emptied all the way out to the bay.

No one for these minutes tried the hot asphalt of the station's entry. The place isolated like a tomb. Then a car, one cop aboard, came down Santa Monica, slewed into the front area of the mission-architecture complex. It braked with black lines on the grey tarmacadam. The uniformed cop threw open his door, painfully reached round, took up a pair of crutches from the rear seat, with difficulty manoeuvred them about and around inside the car, and got them outside, then pulled himself up, staggering to his feet, and slowly made his way into the cop house.

That's something to open up a conversation with a duty sergeant. 'Hey, tell me about your colleague on crutches?' He turned and pulled the keys out of the stream of air, opened the door, gasped as the heat hit, got out fast, and headed across the softened grey tar to the front doors.

Babel inside. Where do you find these Mexican drunks at this hour? And these ones trying to kill each other with oaths in the overtight area behind the duty desk. Fifty people in here, mainly cops, all growling for oxygen from the failing air-conditioning system. No wonder guys died in fights in precinct stations.

There was no choice – a fat sergeant with sweat like black plates under his arms.

'John Dolan.' He flashed his press card quick, as if the rest of him was in that much hurry, and fast answers were the order of the day, and the presses don't wait. '*Village West*.'

'Who's for you?' The fat cop spoke angrily through some broken front teeth, probably a recent subtraction as they hadn't been filed.

'Detective Hagen? I'm a friend of his.'

'Away the day.'

'He said he'd be here, ten.'

'He ain't.'

'Can you find out if he's on patrol?'

'Who says so?'

'No one says so. Could you find out?'

'Why?'

'He said it was important I contact.'

'Write a message. I'll see it gets to him.'

'I know you can rap detective's extension. They'll tell you if he's patrolling.'

'Person, I'm busy. Leave a message.'

'Why d'you think it's not important for you to contact Detective Hagen?'

'Because if it was, person, he'd have a slip in the box.'

The fat sergeant thumbed uninterestedly towards some message cubbyholes.

'And there's no slip in the box?'

'You got it.'

'Why don't you look first before you say that?'

The sergeant's anger was beginning to tighten up a pinkness around his collar. 'Two items, person. One, you're wasting your own time, but that's shit. Two, you're wasting mine. That's bad. Write a message.'

'You've been helpful. People like you make me happy to pay my taxes.'

'Yeah, sure, Fuck you,' the fat cop offered.

Dolan walked out of the babel, back into the burning sun.

It was the wrong time in the morning to be with nothing to do. Bars feckless without custom. Writing a piece was wrong in the heat, the adjectives needed to describe fine wines were precision adjectives, best before nine a.m. Pre-lunch was always overlong sentences with pot-hole syntax. And everybody, that is, the five people he knew in the world, were in work. Twenty million people unemployed, and five in the republic who should be the most unemployable, his friends, all in strait jackets. There was only one place. Dennis Becker would be home, with wife Karen, who would be washing the brown rice for dusk meal, and discussion, and the drinking of foul wine. The kids would be there too, undressed from the waist down, like a cameo out of 'sixties Haight Ashbury.

He checked the gas gauge, still making the calculation, whether to face the Becker household or look at life elsewhere.

He decided. He wanted to check on a girl D.B. had introduced to him a few nights back. An Excise Officer – female. 'This is John Dolan. He's a wine writer, or he's drinking himself to death.'

The Excise Officer had smiled. 'Oh, are you about to get married?'

'Divorced.' D.B. answered for him. 'Try him. Take one of the kid's beds. But don't wake the kids. You're not a screamer? You know why I ask? If you are a screamer and you want to get it on, we'll stay out of the kitchen. As long as you clean up afterwards, you can put Spry on the oil cloth – you know, on the table. I mean, you look like an imaginative gal. I mean if you want to do it on the stairs, I'll just tell the kids to use the other bathroom . . .'

'That's enough,' Dolan had told the little man gently. The lady Excise Officer had started to look grim. D.B. picked up people, male and female, in bars, not for any purpose but that he had a strong initial reaction of liking people, liked asking them what jobs they did, then questions about their working days, habits, in fine detail, then he'd take them back to Karen, who would smile a lot, but didn't give a damn about whether this lady was an Excise Officer currently involved with horse smuggling in from Mexico – or whoever. And then D.B. would drink a lot of cheap wine and get angry with himself, maybe some intuition, fear, that the reason he picked up folk in bars, and brought them home to Karen and brown rice, was that his life was empty, and needed filling up with something, anything, and preferably transient strangers who would never come close enough to him to ask him what he was about. Dolan had liked the blushing Excise Officer. He hoped D.B. had gotten her number.

He drove the Chrysler carefully, eyes squinting

against the sun, down Santa Monica, heading for the ocean. Near its end, in the suburbia behind gas stations, lived D.B. and Karen, where the food bill for cheap wine and a brown rice and salad week came to about the same as a week's rent.

Karen was peeling potatoes. D.B. was writing his novel, the science fiction one. D.B. had never had a novel published, but was writing four of them at once, switching one to another. He'd been writing four novels for about ten years. They were his love story, his sex epic, his biography of Cliff Robertson, and his science fiction epic.

'Hi, Dolan,' he said cheerfully. 'Nice of you to bust in and disturb me.' It was always 'Dolan', never 'John'. 'You're familiar, maybe too familiar, with my Westinghouse – get us a couple.' Beers he meant.

Dolan moved through the mess of the living room, toys, kid's clothes, newspapers, adult sandals, empty glasses, all spread across the board floor. 'Ice in the beer?'

'Maybe,' D.B. answered. He meant when it got too hot the heat exchange of the ancient ice box didn't work.

Karen was at the sink with scraper and potatoes.

'Kiss my neck, John.' She always said this. People in D.B.'s circle kissed a lot – Karen worried always about spreading cold germs to the children.

'What's new?'

'A professor of mine, a friend, walked into the ocean yesterday. It's in the *Times*.'

'Drowned?'

'Right. I thought you didn't eat potatoes.'

'We eat potatoes. Professor where? At Davis?'

'I went to his botany seminar at Davis.'

'Botany, I thought you were oenology studies.'

'Two years ago I was expanding my mind.'

'Does it?'

'A little.'

'So why were you studying botany at an agricultural college?'

'I was studying botany because I was trying to pull Julie and she was studying botany.'

Karen had a question about his ex-wife. 'Have you seen her? Julie?'

'Two months back.'

'How is she?'

'We don't get as far as subtle questions like that. It's money. Questions about money.'

'Well, you shouldn't marry, Dolan, if you're going to divorce someone almost before you get to know them.'

'I got to know her very well. That's where it went wrong. Is that risotto? Potatoes *and* risotto?'

'You're not invited to lunch. You eat too much.' She was smiling.

'I hate the food in this house. Risotto is bad for kids. Let me buy your kids a rib roast.'

'Get out, it's terrific for kids.'

Dolan went back to the living room. D.B. looked up from his mound of manuscripts with a rehearsed faraway look of a major writer returning to the petty world of the living. He took the proffered beer, leant back into the creaking timbers of the one good cane chair. Dolan sank into the fat sofa covered in cat hairs.

'What you at, kid?'

'Fishing and thinking.'

'Oh, that. . .' D.B.'s eyelids hooded, flickered a little, looked back at his manuscript – a second's cameo of uninterest. Then he offered, 'You can help me.' A pause. 'Californian wine. I have to make a purchase.'

'What Californian wine?'

'You know my shit-speak brother – the number-one-son?'

'Tommy?'

'He.' D.B. pursed his lips. 'Yeah. I'm going to hit him for a loan. Five grand. Maybe more. He's got it. He's doing well.'

'I know.'

'He's making more money out of shoes now than before the invention of the automobile. People are walking again.'

'They're unemployed. They can't afford gas.'

'That's terrific news for my brother.' D.B. reached among the literature on the desk and dug out a wine list. 'So asshole's into class Californian of the '77 and '76 vintage.' He handed Dolan the wine list. 'Give me four and I'll make up a mixed case . . .'

Dolan scoured the list. It was reasonable, and the choice was easy. 'This is fine, Chalone Vineyard Pinot Noir, and this, Stony Hill Chardonnay. And here's the best . . .'

'Mark it.'

Dolan took the proffered felt tip. 'Château Montelena Chardonnay.' Dolan marked up the wine, handed the felt tip and the list back.

'Thank you. I don't want you for lunch.'

'Karen's already said I wasn't staying. I want the phone number of the Excise Officer who was here two nights ago.'

'Who he?'

'It was a she. She was beautiful.'

'They're all beautiful. I remember her. I don't have her number.'

'Then you're totally useless.'

'Me? You're getting older, Dolan. You've had the useless life till now – a piece of flotsam on this sea of garbage. I mean how can you afford to waste any more time?'

'I'm working on it.'

'Fuck you for saying that. Don't you understand,

I'm serious?' And suddenly D.B. was serious, blue eyes squinting a line of disapproval to match a frown on his forehead.

'I like my life. Screw you.'

'We're going to have a falling out, you and me.'

Dolan now couldn't figure out whether D.B. was sending him up, or being serious. And for a second he realized D.B. now didn't know either. 'Never. I love your wife too much. And your phone, which I'm going to use.'

He phoned his home number, took a little whistle out of his pocket, and blew the noise. There was a sound of tape rewinding, and the voice of Hagen. 'You missed me at the precinct. Why didn't you stick around? I don't know where I'll be for the rest of the day.'

The second message was from a deeper, more hesitant voice. 'My name is Joseph Stone and I'd very much like to meet you at the earliest convenience. Could you dial me at 246–8841?'

The third message was another from Hagen, 'Maybe do yourself a favour. Phone somebody called Joseph Stone on 246–8841. Talk to you later.'

Dolan dialled the number.

'Yeah . . .' A low voice answered sounding as if it had been weaned reluctantly from sleep.

'Joseph Stone?'

'Yes,' the voice said guardedly.

'John Dolan. I got your message.'

'Yes.' The interception was sharper. 'I'd like to meet you.'

'What's your enquiry?'

There was a pause. 'Let me give you an expensive lunch.'

'When?'

'Now?'

'Okay.'

'What kind of food d'you like to eat?'

Dolan considered the voice had that kind of government employee, cop, official-style monotone. 'I like food in a place with a good wine list.'

'Name it.'

'Caroldi's.' He named the new and most expensive French restaurant in Beverly Hills.

The man let Dolan's three-hundred-dollar challenge be silent on the air a moment. Then he said, matter-of-factly, 'Can you be there in an hour?'

'How will I know you?'

'I'll know you, And . . .' A moment's hesitation as the guy worked out whether to bother to caution the other.

'You'll need a tie.'

'Yeah.' Dolan replaced the phone, turned to D.B. 'A perfect stranger invites me to a three-hundred-dollar lunch.'

D.B. looked up from his manuscript. 'A three-hundred-dollar lunch, and your lousy company, he must want something pretty bad.'

Some light cloud was coming up, attempting to screen off the burning sun, as Dolan walked from Thrifty's parking lot, across Rodeo, and up to Caroldi's. He didn't want to use the parking lot at Caroldi's – a little circumspection about the reaction the battered Chrysler might trigger.

The maitre d' came across yards of expensive gloom and added up the price of Dolan's clothes and shoes in one glance. 'Yes, sir?'

'Mr Joseph Stone arrived?'

'Not yet, sir. If you would perhaps care for a drink?' The maitre d' gestured deep into another cavern of gloom where Dolan's outfit might be more readily camouflaged.

'I need a phone.'

'This way, sir.' The maitre d' led the way to another cavern, walled in black leather and soft light.

'Thank you.' Dolan picked up the phone and dialled the wine store down the street. It was a new store, setting out on a path for chicness. Its list was impressive. 'This is John Dolan. Can I talk to Monsieur Laubenque?'

A moment later a French voice came on the line, harrassed with the all-day detail of trying to make money out of the wine trade. 'Qui?'

'John Dolan.'

'Good afternoon.' The voice controlled itself to politeness.

'You may or may not know of me, I'm the wine correspondent for *Village West*.'

'Yes?' The query was neither an affirmative nor denial.

'Well, I've been writing this month's piece on Rhones and Côte Rôtie, quatre-vingt-huit . . .'

'Oh yes.' The voice was guarded.

'I see you list the Jaboulet Côte Rôtie?'

'That is correct.'

'The fact is I haven't tasted the Jaboulet. I've tasted several others. The Champet, Guignal and Jasmin have for many years been considered the top dogs.'

'Ha!' The Frenchman's voice was derisive.

'However, one always loves the balance of the Jaboulets – in an exceptional year.'

More silence from the Frenchman. Then, 'And you have not tasted the Côte Rôtie?'

'No.' Dolan said, with just enough edge.

'I'd like to note your address and send you a couple of cases. There will be no cost to you.'

'Well, that's very kind,' Dolan offered. 'As it happens, I have some influential friends, fellow wine writers, coming to a little tasting, this week.'

'We could deliver this afternoon.' The Frenchman's voice now sounded slightly grim. Dolan wondered how many other wine writers had hit him for freebie cases recently.

Dolan returned to the bar. The maitre d' approached.

'Mr Stone has arrived.'

A large man stood under the oak beams in the Provençal-style anteroom to the restaurant. He had thick eyebrows over shifting blue eyes, and was wearing an expensive grey suit. His age, Dolan calculated, about forty-eight. He couldn't begin to guess what the guy did for a living. Too expensively dressed for a government official, journalist, or cop. But he must be something official as the contact had come part way through Hagen. A waistcoat went with the suit, and a button above the belly held one end of the gold chain for a Hunter watch. The thing that impressed Dolan about his host was that he looked a hundred per cent fit, and the contrast between himself and the guy, in a Manet-style long mirror, was marked. 'John Dolan?' The big man's voice sounded as if it were venting out of the mouth of an underground cave. 'Joseph Stone. What d'you drink, John?'

'I'll pass. I'll wait for wine.'

'I approve of that. I also approve the restaurant,' the man said expansively.

'Wait for the bill.'

'Quality you pay for.'

A waiter approached offering leather-bound menus. The large man waved him aside. 'We'll go straight to our table. A quiet one,' he added the man's name, 'François . . .'

So Stone knew the waiters by name.

Dolan had thought the restaurant empty, but now as they pierced the gloom and entered the low room he saw folk in coverts, voices quietened by thick silk walls and deep carpets. The indefinable smell of fine cuisine, simmering Normandy butter, and fresh flowers, assailed him as he followed the fit tread of his host and maitre d' far across the restaurant to a corner, hooded by a round pergola of high-back seating and more curtains.

'Mr Stone, is this for you satisfactory?'

The big man gave table and flatware and curtains the once-over with a look of half pleasure, half doubt.

'Fine.'

'Thank you, Monsieur. I will send the menus.'

The menus arrived. 'Okay, John. I'll be eating a steak. I'll start with some oysters. Choose the wine.'

'Yeah?'

'Order what you want.' He said it in a voice that suggested he wasn't paying for it either.

Dolan studied the wine list, aware that Stone's eyes were searching his face for some clue to an opening sentence to explain the lunch invitation. 'You went to this wine college?'

'Davis College.'

'Where you get to study wine, right?'

'Right.'

'And you work for *Village West*?'

'Currently.'

A waiter was hovering, doing a little sullen arabesque of not quite ignoring them while flicking crumbs off a nearby table.

'What wine strikes your fancy?' Stone asked.

'Two-hundred-and-ten-dollars' worth of Marey Monge Romanee Conti '69.'

Stone shrugged with a slight smile. 'Are you going to eat as well?'

'I'll have the lamb Reforme. After pâté de foie.'

Stone's eyes went back to the menu, maybe to check those prices. He shrugged. 'Sure.'

They ordered.

The wine arrived with a sommelier who had received his training at La Scala, Milan. They got Act Three where a nectar of the gods is dispensed to some dying soprano. But he didn't muff the decanting to a Baccarat decanter.

Stone started into his oysters as soon as they arrived – an implicit gesture of eat now, talk later. The questions came as Dolan put a first fork into the lamb.

'John, at Davis, you were taught by a guy who died, Leon Markovicz?'

'Died yesterday.'

'Right. Can you tell me about him?'

The mouthful of lamb had precedence over an instant answer. He took his time swallowing. 'Sure. What d'you want to know?'

'Give me some background.'

'What sort of background?'

'What did you know of Markovicz' life?'

'Polish Jew. Studied in Vienna, Yale, M.I.T. On the surface a kind of mark one crazy professor. That's what he gave out. I don't know if it was real.'

'Why d'you say that?'

Dolan considered. How much should he tell this man in exchange for an expensive lunch? 'He was a genius biologist. I understand he was kind of kicked out of M.I.T.'

'Right.'

'His talents were hardly used at Davis.'

'How's that?'

'He conducted an optional course in root stock studies, hybridization. It wasn't an essential course for oenological studies.'

'Oenological studies is studying about wine?'

'Yes.'

'Tell me about him, as a lecturer.'

'Well, anyone will tell you he was a complicated man.'

'Complicated how?'

'Sometimes he cried in lectures.'

'Cried?' Stone echoed the word vaguely as if he'd already heard it used in the context of the professor. 'You and your wife were personal friends of the professor?'

'Ex-wife.'

'Have you spoken to Mrs Markovicz since yesterday – the drowning?'

'No, I will do.'

'Tell me about her.'

Dolan sipped the expensive wine, and couldn't think of any reason not to. 'She lost her parents, all her family, in concentration camps. She's been arrested in L.A. a few times. She found some chapter of the Ku Klux Klan, their addresses in Los Angeles. She went to the addresses, threw bricks through their windows. Screamed at them about Klansmen being the heirs to Hitler. She did all this when she was drunk. Anybody who made a right-wing remark in her company was called a "Nazi". She obviously didn't, doesn't, endear herself – like to other faculty members where Leon worked.'

Stone took in the information with a series of little nods. He had stopped eating, placed his knife and fork parallel on his plate. 'You've been very forthcoming, John.'

'I've told you what's common knowledge. Now I have to ask, what's this lunch?'

Stone shrugged as if Dolan's question was a small irrelevance that had somehow crept in to disturb a train of thought. Across the restaurant a man laughed, and Stone turned and gave a glance through the gloom as if the person was somehow laughing at him. He turned back, put the tips of his fingers together, offered a confidential look. 'You're a nice guy, John Dolan. I ran a check.'

'Ran a check?'

'A man of twenty-seven. You've never been in real trouble with the cops. Good background. Your dad was in the army. Right? Then a farmer. Right? It's a difficult time in this society for people to be scrupulous. You are. You're an honest man, It's rare.'

'Depends on who you meet, Mr Stone.'

'All kinds. Now – the only small criticism is – you want to hear it?'

'Let's hear it.'

'You haven't done a lot with your talents.'

'That a fact?'

'Right.'

'I'm Leo Tolstoy. Later, rather than sooner, the world will have my *War and Peace*.'

Stone was nodding, but Dolan didn't know if it was approval, or a nod at the ease of the excuse for his sloth.

'So you're going to write a novel?'

'Perhaps.'

'So if I put fifty grand your way, maybe that would aid the process of your starting to do your serious thing?'

Dolan let the statement float for a moment. He sipped the deep, mouth-filled Marey Monge. 'Fifty grand?'

'Yes.'

'For what?'

'It would be in cash. You don't have to declare it to the Internal Revenue.'

'But you say I'm a good guy.'

'Cash is cash, John.'

'Cash for what?'

Stone took out a cigar case, opened it. 'May I offer you?'

'Thank you, no.'
'Do you smoke?'
'The occasional cigarette.'
Stone took his time lighting the cigar, a dozen practised small puffs until the end was well alight. 'Look, getting a wine degree at Davis, I mean, it's a highly technical subject, it's the sort of thing where if you go for a degree, and then want to go on into the wine trade, you'd keep all your college notes. Right?'
'Right,' said Dolan.
Stone exhaled a small cloud of smoke. He leaned forward as if about to give, or seek, a confidence. 'Now, John Dolan, did you take notes on Markovicz' lectures, and, more to the point, did you keep them?'
'I took them. I think I kept them.'
'Think?' Stone questioned the word.
'A lot of my stuff is with my ex-wife. She got the house. She studied with me. I'm sure she'd know not to throw my Davis College stuff away. But who knows?'
'Can you find out?'
'I can. Why?'
'I'm prepared to pay you fifty thousand dollars for your notes on Professor Markovicz' lectures.'
Dolan let it roll over him. The guy was either mad or had some real motive he couldn't immediately guess at. 'Now, Mr Stone, here's point one. I took lecture notes – this sounds crazy, but I really didn't understand most of what Leon was saying. I had some elemental botany. Markovicz was an almost impossible lecturer to follow. But I liked him for the qualities most people probably detested him for – sadness, vulnerability, incompetence, hopelessness . . .'
'You can stop there, John.' Stone made it sound generous, paternal. 'The important thing is you may have somewhere notes on Markovicz' lectures. I'll give you fifty grand for them. There's one proviso.'

'What's that?'

'It's your next question. You'll want to ask me why I'm prepared to pay high for a bunch of notes?'

'Yes.'

'The proviso is you don't get an answer. I'm going to write down a number, John, where you can phone me. When you can show me you've got Markovicz' notes I'll come round with a bag of money . . .'

Dolan lived in a peeling white pile in Venice – Venice was his address though it was Santa Rosa Boulevard where, just when they were needed, the cooling inshore breezes seemed to give up as they hit the first cluster of gas stations of Seventh Street.

Dolan's father had been a professional soldier first, then a farmer. He was a humourless man, cold in disappointment. The army career had retired him at captain's rank instead of colonel, which he stated he should have got. He brooded on this. Later, the farm gave problems, not large enough at four hundred acres of grain to be an economic unit. He had died three years back. He left his little goods and chattels to Dolan's mother who blew it all on drink.

Dolan's father had been six feet two, Dolan himself just under six. His mother was a tiny woman, stretched out on the floor drunk she took up less than five feet of carpet. After the move to Venice, the mother stopped drinking for a few months while she set about buying furniture for the house. And as she was a little woman, she filled the house with little furniture. Little chairs and tables, little clocks (a 'grandmother' clock in the hall), little vases with little plants in them, little pots and pans in the little kitchen. The only things to scale with normalcy in the house – no miniaturization here – were the scotch glasses, a full eight ounces.

She had died of cirrhosis two years ago, almost on

the anniversary of his dad's death through disappointment. Dolan had lived on alone in this house. The place depressed him so much he couldn't even face the prospect of thinking long and hard enough about it to organize selling it.

He got back from the Stone lunch and checked his message machine. Hagen's voice came on, 'Hi. I'll get back to you sometime today.'

Dolan groaned. He wanted to talk to Hagen about Stone.

He dialled his ex-wife up at Napa. He was at a loss for a moment when she answered the phone. Somehow he hadn't expected her to be in. 'Julie, it's me.'

'Yes?' The word said flatly, with no interest or emphasis.

'Listen, this is important. You still got the trunks?'

'Your tin trunks?'

'Right.'

'In the garage.'

'You never threw anything away – anything that was in my trunks?'

'No,' She said this word as if he'd been talking for an hour and she'd reached the state beyond boredom.

'Can I drive up tonight?'

'No.'

'Why not?'

'I have friends. I don't want you around.'

'I'll come up tomorrow.'

'I may not be around.'

'I want to collect my trunks.'

'They've been bitching up the garage for two bastard years. And you with all that goddam room in Venice.'

'See you.' He put the phone down gently on any further protest.

The two gift cases of Côte Rôtie which he'd wangled before the Stone lunch had been waiting on his porch when he got back – an impressive service. He took the wine in, and downstairs into a shuttered basement room which he used as his cellar. He opened one bottle, but it would have to breathe for two, three hours before he tasted it. In the middle of the room, surrounded by ceiling-high piles of freebie wine cases, there was a table, desk lamp and a chair. He sat down and started to write the Rhone article which he'd told the new wine shop he'd finished. Later he'd go to D.B.'s and discuss the Stone offer with him. D.B. was essentially a hood in sheep's clothing. He'd have some ideas on Stone and his proposition.

D.B. was high on chemical compounds or alcohol or both, and his views on Stone and current world problems were noisy and confused. There were a few people in the house, including a go-go dancer. Dolan and Karen retired to the kitchen with the kids, and Dolan got drunk.

He got back to his house about midnight and went straight to bed.

He came painfully out of a deep stupor of sleep around two a.m. The front door bell was ringing. At the same time the door knocker banged urgently. He lurched out of his bed, fumbled a light switch, checked his alarm clock. He wrestled with a dressing-gown over his nakedness, cursed, set off on an erratic course down the stairs, to the front door and, angry, pulled it open.

'John . . .' She nearly fell into the hall, recovered herself, opened her legs to get a better stance, stood there, hands on hips, face flushed, drunk, with an aggressive expression.

Mrs Leon Markovicz was wearing a black cocktail

dress, no shoes. One of the straps of the dress was broken – the shaped material had fallen over her left breast revealing one cup of a heavy duty, cheap bra. Dolan looked from the flushed face to the breast, with a thought that he'd had on other occasions. She must be near fifty, but she still had the body of a young woman.

'What do you want?'

She swung a small black cocktail bag in one hand. She looked as if she'd come from some wild party. 'Haven't you heard? Leon's drowned . . .' She said it as if it was the reason why she'd been to a party.

'Yes. I heard. Read it.'

'I gotta talk to you.' The voice as usual the mix of something like Pittsburgh over a thicker Central European accent.

'It's two in the morning.' Dolan stood his ground, though he wanted her in. He wanted to ask her some questions, but not when she was drunk.

'So you work in Amtrak? You gotta be up at five?' A possible explanation came over her expression in an oily grin. 'Oh, I see. You're with woman? That's okay. Give me a drink. I'll wait.'

He gave up. 'Come in.' He stood back. She fell forward. He grabbed her, but with a sudden sharp strength she pulled away.

'Now wait a minute, John Dolan . . .' Eyes narrowed, mouth tightened to a snap. 'You think I'm here for that.' She almost spat her conclusion in his face.

She was off, wavering at her own pace down the hall, and colliding with the upright of a door. He followed her into the kitchen, beat her to the light switch, just before she rammed into the breakfast bar.

'Mrs Markovicz . . .' He felt his voice getting tense.

'Greta. Jesus sake!' A cackle of laughter mixed with the remonstrance. 'Hey, I'll put some coffee on.'

'Greta. I was asleep. You probably woke every neighbour in the street. What can I do for you?'

'Leon's dead.' Suddenly she looked helpless, broken.

'I know, I'm very sorry.'

'You think I wander the night? Any shit place? Wake people up?' She checked the water level in the kettle, then switched it on. 'You wanna digress on the semiology of "help", "trouble"? Where d'ya keep your coffee?' She started blundering down a row of cupboards, pulling doors open.

'I'll do it,' he said sharply. 'You sit down.' The order made her halt. She turned, gave him a cold look, moved backwards to a bar stool, sat, slid, almost fell off it – recovered herself.

Dolan found the instant coffee, set out two cups.

'You gotta drink?'

'I think you should have coffee.'

'You think I've had too much. Say it . . .'

'I don't want to start drinking at two a.m.'

'You know something?' She looked at him speculatively. 'I bet you think you're someone – you're terrific. You know the only lay in this town worth having is a U.S. Marine? Over and over and over they do it. Desperation. Marines are like us, the Jews. No, not you. You're no Jew. You couldn't be.'

'Where are you staying in town?'

'All Nazis are asparagus tips. The creed – impotence. Führer with a little moustache – anti-phallic symbol. I'm not calling you a Nazi.' She qualified it. 'I don't think you are a Nazi. All of us have got a little Nazi in us.' She grimaced, coughed, spluttered.

'Greta, why have you come here?'

'You want it?'

'I want it.'

'Somebody tried to kill me this afternoon.' Now

she bowed her head as if by concentrating on the floor she'd find some clearer way of explaining herself.

'Kill you?'

'Was in the Killanin Library, U.C.L.A. Checking maybe Leon left some papers there. I come out. I go to the parking lot. There's a big guy, never seen him before. Well, maybe I do, but you know – things are vague. Ten years of living with Leon. Listen, J. Dolan,' she was looking at him critically, testing for a sympathy which was not yet there – somebody tried to kill me.'

'You're telling me.'

'He drove his car right at me. I hear screams. Should have been my screams. But it's behind – you know, way back. He's coming at me. I turn to look for the screams. It's three girl students. I'm looking at them. They're screaming because I'm about to get run down. I turn back. I leap to the side. He just misses me.'

Every instinct told him, she's too drunk now to handle questions, about being run at with a car, about Leon, about the drowning, about Stone, and why Leon's lecture notes should be worth money.

'The three – the girls, took me home. You're looking at me like I'm in a strait jacket. It's verifiable phenomena.'

'You phoned the cops?'

'No.'

'Why not?'

'Who murders more people in this nation than anyone else? Look at the blacks, in prison. They die, you know. The cops kill them. No one says anything. No one speaks out.'

'It's jailors who kill blacks in prison.'

'Says you. Hitler is alive in your silence!' She was working herself into an anger.

Dolan let a little silence float, wondered what to make of her presence and her story.

'In my bag. They wrote it down. The girls wrote down their names, addresses. It's proof positive.'

'Look, why would someone try to run you down?' He was still distanced from her hysteria, uncertain, maybe the oncoming car was a blown up incident as exaggerated as her Nazi fixations. 'Why would somebody try to attack you?'

'Why d'you use the word "attack"? Say it – murder me!'

'Okay, look, why are you here? Why have you come here?'

Her reply was fast. 'It's got to be – it's got to relate to Leon. They want his papers. They want everything he ever wrote. They want everything he ever said. They want every note anybody ever took down. They want the total legacy of Leon Markovicz.' She fell silent into some private extension of her thoughts. 'Well, you know all this.'

Dolan didn't. 'What do I know?'

'Stone told me. You could be selling to him – the notes of Leon's lectures. I told Stone to shove his head up his ass! Maybe a dozen hours later someone comes at me. I mean I'm not going to put up with you, J. Dolan.'

'Put up with what?'

'Did you get it – fifty grand?'

'Not yet.'

'How dare you.' Her voice was now rising. 'Those notes are my husband's life. Never yours to possess . . . Jesus!'

She was on her feet now, moving forward, raising her arms as if about to attack him.

'Shut up! Sit down!' He pitched the command as a threat.

She seemed to take a second look at him, another

calculation, her temper suddenly evaporating to calm. 'May I use your phone?'

'Help yourself.'

She staggered across to the wall phone, wrestled with her black bag, took out a piece of paper, studied it, dialled. A silence. Then her voice exploded into a welcoming, 'Hi! I'm Mrs Markovicz. I want you to tell a jerk here about the bastard tried to run me down. U.C.L.A. Come on, girlie,' sharper now, 'this is important . . . I don't care what the goddam time is . . .'

Dolan could hear protests from the other end of the line.

'Come on! All you have to say to this asparagus tip is a guy tried to kill me, you know?' She turned and imperiously held the phone out to Dolan.

He groaned, stepped forward. 'I didn't say I didn't believe you.'

'You implied with your creepy expression.'

He took the phone, spoke into it. 'I'm sorry you've been disturbed. . . '

Mrs Markovicz exploded, screamed at the kitchen wall. 'He's sorry to disturb some shit student! I nearly got murdered!'

The girl student was hardly awake. 'We saw a black car. Didn't see much of the guy. But he was a big guy . . . well, he ran at the lady. And we all screamed and he drove away . . . That's it . . .'

'Thanks,' Dolan replaced the phone.

She looked triumphant. 'You, me and your shitty wife – my husband's work. You're going to help me. I mean, you know how to talk to Nazis. I mean I don't care Stone is buying you off. All I want to know is why? And who he works for. In other words, who wants me out of the way. You're going to do this, and today.'

'It's two o'clock in the morning, Greta.'

'I don't care what time it is. You're going to help

me. I don't want to let you out of my sight. I have to stay here.'

'Here?'

'I can sleep on a chair. No funny business now.' She made the sentence a sneer.

He was lost for a decision. It arrived by default. He hadn't the energy to argue her out of the house. 'Go sleep on the divan next door – and let me sleep. Okay. We'll sort this out in the morning.'

'Deal.' She headed for the front door.

'Where are you going?'

'My dog. You want him to spend the night in a Jeep?'

Dolan groaned, remembering the Markovicz dog, a huge French hunting poodle – the kind of dog that needs fifteen miles exercise over Provençal hills every day. 'I don't want the dog in my house.'

But she was gone at sprint pace out of the front door. A moment later he heard yelps, followed by basso profundo growls and the animal bounded in, hauling Mrs Markovicz in its wake.

'Sit. Shut up! Cesar, shut up!'

The dog ignored her, jerked its neck on the lead so hard it flew from her hand. It rocketed out of the kitchen and headed down the hall to somewhere, and silence.

'He'll settle down,' she said hopelessly. 'Go on. Go on. Get your precious sleep . . .'

Dolan eventually found sleep. The dog had taken up residence in the bedroom opposite his own, and it snored. He was beyond care, didn't give a damn when he next heard noises of banging pots, cooking, from below. He slept till six o'clock, fell into another deep asleep until eight o'clock, wakening with a start. The house was silent. He went downstairs.

She was gone, but she'd left the huge poodle. It growled at him blamefully as he stepped into the kitchen. It was tethered by its lead to the Frigidaire door.

Dolan had a small wardrobe. Two winter outfits. Blue denim suit, bought in New York, which could be washed in a laundromat and pulled on a hanger back to shape. Eight pairs of jeans, all dark green, a plaid English sports jacket and a dozen wool check shirts.

Over the years he had given his appearance some thought – some self-discipline against an urge always to dress down towards dropping out. Around his neck, year long, on a tight silver chain, hung a small American Indian flat jade carving of a bull's head, face on – a gift from a New York girl he had lived with for three weeks behind silted windows in Cornelia Street.

The second winter outfit was a Missoni suit, another gift from a girl who was in the rag trade. The suit was three years old. A year after getting the suit he'd met Julie. 'Terrific suit,' Julie had said the first time she saw it. 'Here, put these earrings in your pocket.'

'Crazy thing is, there are no pockets,' Dolan had told her. 'Missoni suit – supposed to be the best, and no pockets – they're dummies.'

'They can't be,' she had said.

Somebody had forgotten to remove the tailor's tacking – the pockets had been tacked closed for a year. So he'd worn a Missoni suit thinking, 'What a hype, no pockets.' There were nine pockets in the suit.

He dressed in it to go and face Julie. Julie had a habit of treating him like a bum – he would turn up looking sharp. He took a long time to get the tie right, and find matching socks. Then he checked the result in the mirror, said half aloud, 'Fuck it.' He went downstairs and fed the French poodle some packet ham slices and went out to the car.

The Pacific Coast Highway was full of sun and

threat. He'd noticed before, the coast road to San Francisco was paved with motorists of two different identities. One lot, Sunday style, laid back at wheel of camper or Ford Limited, with kids hanging out, the second, waves of missile mobiles killing up the coast, wedged with drug-crazed no-accounts, their molls, and their closed-eyed, cop-shooting friends. This morning the second grouping had taken over the road. The Chrysler was soon close to running out of brakes. Foot-stamping precision was needed, expertise on ball of toe with accelerator, and hard stamp on heel on clutch and brake. The stick shift had developed a life of its own – its vital ball about to fall off, and a noise like an Italian castrato coming up from the direction of the gears. He arrived in the outskirts of San Francisco at three p.m., drained, exhausted. He pulled into a gas station. A student-type guy stepped out and, looking the smoking Chrysler over, asked to see cash before he let Dolan fill up. It was a small insult but somehow a final straw. Dolan paid, and called the guy 'a cunt' to his face. The guy shrugged – the word overused in the world of gas stations, now weakened of meaning, debased, devoid of provocation.

He took a cross-town route and picked up Highway 121 on its exit flight from the bay. Suburbs next, of gas stations, hyper-markets, motels and house-of-cards housing, up to the sprawled blight of Vallejo and then on to 29, and the first hesitation of hills. Napa next, and the start of the seas of vineyards, the air now smelling of sea although the Pacific was some miles away.

He'd been driving this route now for six years. The changes in Napa had transformed it. It had become, in just the last four years, like a huge construction site for vines, and it had been the construction-site millionaires, like Phelps, who had remade it. At last he saw, just off the highway, the signs for the Carneros Creek Winery and slowed into the right lane. Julie lived in a house that Dolan had described as a 'shack' when he'd lived there. The construction material was termite-infested wood. All traces of the white paint that had once covered it had now disappeared. The house had come with Julie and the marriage, and she had wanted them to live there. It had become a running sore. Julie was sure it could be refurbished. Dolan had argued the only way to initiate that was to pull it down, and start again. Julie loved the house – and as it turned out, her feelings for it were stronger than for him. It was approached by a broken pathway lined with olive trees, unpruned for years, and now out of control. To one side of the roadside verge house entrance was a twenty-foot hoarding for MOBIL OIL.

He rang the doorbell. He heard some movement from the other side of the door, and then a man's voice. 'Who is it?'

'It's me, John.'

'Who is you?'

'Is Julie there?'

The door opened and Dolan nearly took a step back at the sight of the apparition. He was about eighteen, in a jockstrap, grey with dirt, and an Indian shawl around his shoulders, and nothing else. A thin, emaciated body was so stooped forward that it was difficult to gauge the boy's height, which might be nearly six feet. It was the eyes and hair that shocked Dolan. The eyes seemed to be on the point of falling out of their sockets, the pupils dilated into black discs – Dolan knew it was dope, and something powerful.

'May I ask who you are?'

The creature wavered forward, looked close into Dolan's face as if the answer to the question might be there. The boy had obviously set about his hair or head with an open razor. Then he'd dyed the remaining dirty hanks with green, blue and yellow tints. The razor had cut random paths down to bare shining skull below.

'Julie? She's playing chess,' the house guest managed to articulate.

'Who are you?'

The boy looked confused. He didn't know any more.

Dolan got back in the car and drove into Napa, and headed for Malcolm's Wine bar.

It was on two floors, and architecturally was supposed to be a copy of some Rothschild chais. On the bottom floor, to one side of some giant barrels, there was a line of eight card tables. On each table a chess board, and at each table a chess gambler, age twenty to seventy. Julie moved from table to table. She had a sheaf of ten-dollar bills in her left hand and paused perhaps thirty seconds at each table to make her chess move. At one table the chess gambler wanted to raise his stake, and she agreed. Dolan's eyes went up and down the tables, calculating. If she won all ten games, and she ought to – she was good – then the eight stakes must add up to over five hundred dollars.

She looked up from a board as he came downstairs, straight at him, without reaction. He took a seat and waited.

He always felt some tug when he saw her, as now, after an absence. He'd married her because she'd represented anarchy, personal courage, ability to deal with anybody and any situation. She had survived her life up to that point, untamed, unshackled by society. She was a free spirit, and clever, or maybe brilliant. She only had to decide and she could do anything she wanted. She had direction. Or that was what he'd thought.

And then they were married and she told him – told him she'd married him because she'd thought he was so straight, ambitious, would make money. He couldn't believe she'd got him so wrong. How could a brilliant girl make such a miscalculation?

The last time he'd seen her was six weeks ago – the visit with Markovicz and Greta to the Hunt house, for the juggling episode.

The wait ran to half an hour. But he was enjoying watching her play. She was a winner, at chess. All the other games in life, like breeding, loving, finding happiness, she had been born to lose at. And somehow the thrust of the marriage, when she realized he wasn't going to save her, had been that he must lose as well. He must never assume in her presence that he was more than just garbage. He must never correct, criticize, demand or decree. He must go humbled into her arena for the fight, where she was both champion and referee.

She picked up the last of her winnings and came across to him. 'You look a mess. The Missoni doesn't hide anything.'

'Sure.' He shrugged his uninterest in her verdict.

'You want a wine?'

'Not here.'

'They got a good Clos du Val. Cheap.'

'Coffee maybe? At the house?'

'Drive me. I had to sell the Pinto.'

'Why?'

'Beyond repair.'

They went out into the sun. She ran her eye over the Chrysler. 'You know something . . .'

'What?'

'This car. The tastelessness of your perpetual poverty is sickening.' She got in.

'I just want my Markovicz lecture notes.'

'You're goddam lucky I didn't throw your stuff in

the incinerator a year back. You with all that room in Venice.'

'You mentioned that.'

'I mention it again.' She was glaring at him now. 'So when are you going to get to the point?'

'What point?'

'You know, you're a real jerk. The point, jerk, is that you've had some approach from a guy called Stone to sell your Markovicz lecture notes. Now why didn't you tell me that?'

'I was going to.'

'Maybe you weren't.'

'So Stone's approached you?'

'Stone's approached me.'

'What have you told him?'

'What I told him, tell him, doesn't concern you. But I looked through the tin trunks and I found your notes, and my notes. You have eleven notebooks.'

'Eleven?' Dolan was surprised by the number.

'Right.'

'So you don't want to tell me what you're saying to Stone?'

'No.' She said it businesslike.

'Okay.'

As he turned the Chrysler up past the Mobil sign he asked her, 'Who's the freak in the dirty grey jockstrap and the part-shaved skull?'

'Freak?'

'Yes,' he said sharply.

'To you of the Missoni, he's a freak. But he cares for me.'

'How old is he? Eighteen? Nineteen?'

'Who cares?'

'How much does it cost you to keep him in elephant tranquilliser?'

'He works. He's got a regular job.'

'Where would he work, looking like that, without being arrested?'

'He's a butcher.'

'Butcher?' Dolan was more surprised than amused.

'At least he brings home fresh meat. We always got fresh meat in the house. Unlike my time with you. All you could razzle up was cases of wine that was freebie because it was so lousy.'

'In those days, wine was important. You were a drunk, remember?'

They got out of the car. 'Do me a favour,' she said. 'Skip the coffee. Take your lecture notes, and go. I got 'em ready in the kitchen.'

'Sure.'

They went in. The boy with the part-shaved head, now without the shawl, was lying on the floor in a corner of the kitchen. She went over to him, knelt down and angled his face around, to check his breathing. Satisfied, she got up, went across to a cupboard, took out a brown paper package. 'Your pads.'

Dolan took the package. 'What about him? You want I lift him up to the bedroom?'

'No, he's okay. He sleeps on the floor.'

'Has he got a name?'

'Why?'

'I'd like to talk to him sometime. Recommend my barber.'

'His name's Matisse.'

'Christian name, or surname?'

'Both. It's the name of the Parisian artist. He's also an artist.'

The boy on the floor stirred and gave a rattling cough.

'You're waking him. Don't.'

At the door he turned. 'You don't want to get together with me on the business of Stone? We might find out more, working together.'

'No,' she said sharply. 'I'll handle it myself. You handle yourself. The days of you fucking me up are over.'

'Okay, but don't you want to know why he's trying to buy our notebooks?'

She paused to consider. 'You know something? I think he's genuine. I don't give a monkey's pratt what he wants the notebooks for if he's coming across with some dough . . .'

He'd met Detective Don Hagen four years before in a place west on Sunset Strip which couldn't make up its mind if it was a bar, a restaurant, or a clip joint. It was a first visit to the place by Dolan. No one seemed to be eating in the restaurant. He was there to drink wine, and get drunk, and move on. A heavy-built man in an electric blue suit came in with a blonde on his arm. This was Hagen. The bar had twenty people in it all morose and contained. Hagen and the girl were expansive, on the way to getting well liquored, but looking around to chalk up a few social contacts.

Dolan had asked for some wine at the bar. A week-old third of a bottle of Almedan was produced, tasted by Dolan, and rejected. 'It's a dead man. It's oxidized,' he told the barman.

The barman demurred, insisted the bottle was fresh at lunch. Hagen came in on it. 'Let me taste. Give me a glass.' The barman poured, Hagen sipped and grimaced. 'It's a corpse,' he told the barman. 'I know my wines.'

He did. He abandoned the blonde for a half hour as he put his head together with Dolan. As soon as Dolan told him he'd gone on the wine course at Davis, Hagen was all ears. They swapped some chat on California makers and vintages.

'Mount Veeder Winery,' Hagen said.

'It doesn't get credit enough. Especially the '77's.'

'I had 'em all since '74. Got a few cases of '77 laid down. The rub, old pal, will they make it through the next few years to my old age when I'll need the bastards?'

'I always think they balance good too young.'

A large quantity of booze passed quickly through the gesticulating hands of the detective. He'd now introduced himself as a cop. Dolan had cooled a little – but alcohol warmed him up again to the man in the blue suit, with a blonde who was now passing out. Her name was Mildred.

Dandruff began to appear on the electric blue collar – Dolan spotted it – a sure sign of an alcoholic. And Hagen was beginning to stoop – his near six feet now bent to lose six inches as he stood wavering, giving loud-voiced orders, making poor jokes, and reminiscing about wine. Dolan decided he should leave before Hagen and the girl had heart attacks on the basis of what they had consumed. Others from the bar were leaving as Hagen's voice pitched higher.

'I have to leave,' Dolan announced.

'You can't! You're my new pal. You're gonna eat.' Hagen had indicated the half-lit restaurant, now boasting two diners. The three fell into seats in the restaurant. A silence now came to the table. Mildred, pie-eyed with drink. Hagen glowering at a menu. Dolan looking at the lousy wine list. Dolan felt no constraint to puncture it. Mildred had then suddenly made a number of small sniffing noises that sounded like a preparation for tears, a comment either on her drunken condition, or perhaps her relationship to Hagen. Hagen either ignored the sniffs or didn't hear them.

'It's cold, isn't it?' Hagen had looked up at Dolan. It was as if he was searching for some general statement about the weather – as if he was so out of it he'd forgotten the season and needed reminding, like for Dolan to say, 'No, it's hot. It's summer.'

Dolan had said nothing, but felt the beginnings of the sense of being trapped for the evening by the cop and his moll.

'You okay?' Hagen had asked.

'I'm okay,' Dolan had offered guardedly. There was a sense of foreboding now settling around the night, the feel of a foul meal about to be further ruined – an unpleasantness rising at the table, and Dolan's own inability to do anything about it.

'What paper d'you work for?' Hagen had asked.

'*Village West.*'

Four large men had entered from the street, passed the bar up, and come into the restaurant. Dolan had given them a quick appraisal. They were hugely built, looked like professional athletes. They spoke quietly to each other as they settled on a table across the small room. They then went quiet. They were looking at Mildred. Mildred was still crying, getting drunker. The straps that held her dress up had begun to slide off the shoulders. Neither Hagen nor she had yet noticed.

Then Hagen noticed. 'See these guys.' He seized Dolan by the shoulder and pointed. 'See 'em, eyes stuck out like penises, looking at her. Jesus, what shit . . They have not once taken their eyes off her fuckin' tits . . .'

The big guys were ten feet away, but sitting ten yards away they still would have heard the volume. It could only be deliberate. Hagen poured out more obscenity. Dolan watched the guys and listened to it. Mildred was too gone to see the danger.

It took three minutes of insult, and then the four guys had got up and come over. From the time they arrived at the table events happened fast.

Dolan felt himself lifted out of his seat and propelled backwards across the restaurant, through the bar, past the vacant frozen faces of astonished drinkers.

Seconds later he and Hagen were in the street, and the guys were pounding them, fists and feet.

Dolan had fought like an animal, suddenly realizing that these guys were so powerful it might be his life at stake. They took their time. They beat him and Hagen to a pulp in a leisured, mechanical way. They broke one of Hagen's wrists, a thumb, two ribs, and split an eyebrow fifteen stitches in length. Dolan was held upright as they punched him. Then he went down. He passed out as they kicked him.

He came to, ten, fifteen minutes later. The four were gone. There were plenty of people around but standing well back. Mildred was sitting on the restaurant stoop crying hysterically. Hagen was face down in the gutter vomiting. Dolan had looked down at his clothes. He'd already emptied his stomach. Hagen got up on his knees, turned round slowly, face seared with pain. 'You were terrific, kid . . . Jesus, d'you pack a left! Terrific! Jesus you were terrific . . .'

Hagen had got it all wrong. Dolan didn't remember packing any left. But the cop had decided he'd put a monstrous attack on the four. Well, Dolan reassured himself, the fact was he could have tried to run and he didn't. The upshot was Hagen had decided Dolan was a hero. 'Any time I can do something for you . . .' Hagen had promised. He'd repeated the promise and proved useful many times.

Hagen lived in a condominium, four years old, on San Vincente – he'd just moved in around the time of the bar fight. It was an apartment which then had cost him over a hundred and fifty thousand and a few tongues must have wagged at Beverly Hills P.D. 'My uncle died and left me some scratch,' Hagen had explained.

The first time Dolan visited the place it was still unpainted. It had a bed, but no furniture. There was a second bedroom with some cases of wine spread about. Hagen's clothes were hung on metal hangers from every door handle in the place. Four years later, there was still really no furniture, and the door knobs were still heavy with the hangers. 'Look at it this way, when I go to put this on the market, it's still a new apartment – the guy coming in has got an untouched place. Besides, I hardly live here – it's only a bed, and a broad, in the dawn.'

Dolan, back from Napa, called Hagen's answering machine to leave a message. He was surprised when Hagen, voice bright and peppery, answered.

'It's me, John.'

'Been trying to get you,' Hagen said. 'Come over. Split a bottle. I got the day off. I'm thinking about a jag. It's been time since I indulged.'

Hagen's 'jags' lasted three days of solid drinking. Dolan debated the idea. He didn't want to get swallowed up in one of them. Hagen was an attritive host – once you accepted the first bottle, it became a contract to get on the conveyor line.

'One bottle.'

'Screw,' Hagen remonstrated cheerfully. 'By the way, I got some good news, but mostly bad news for you.'

Dolan drove to San Vincente through the clearing air of a morning drop in temperature, and the stirring of breezes inshore.

Hagen greeted him in a T-shirt and torn jeans. Dolan realized the cheerful voice on the phone was a minute's aberration, he'd clearly been on the booze last night – the assault had drained him of colour, put a fine film of sweat on forehead, a tremble in the hand offering a glass of red wine, and still some slur in speech.

'What time is it? I seem to have lost my watch, and also, my goddam shoes. I think they're down your way, near the ocean.'

Dolan checked his watch. 'It's ten, around. Were you asleep when I rang?'

'I don't know,' Hagen said tired-voiced, and turned and headed into the grey cement wall area of space which in other apartments was a living room. A table, imported since the last time Dolan had been there, had now joined two wooden chairs as the total triumvirate of contents. Six open red wines and six relatively clean glasses awaited the tasting.

'This is – I got hold of some of this overpriced shit – David Bruce Winery – Zinfandel '78. Tell me.' He poured a sample for Dolan.

'I don't want to drink much. I'm saying that definite to you.'

'Who needs you?' Hagen said it back slyly.

'I know the '78. A little over heavy, usually sophisticated, lack of roundness.'

'Maybe.' Hagen tried a sip. 'Now whose problems do we talk of – me or yours first?'

'You.'

Six months ago Hagen had been out on patrol, and had got a call to go to a building site on Lindacrest Drive – stolen truck spotted on the site. Hagen had driven into the site, approached a construction worker's wood hut – called out. A guy had stepped out and taken a shot at him. Hagen had emptied his revolver into the wood hut. Inside another man died, and was posthumously alibied. The problem for Hagen was that this was a dead ringer scenario for something that had happened six years previously – two guys had died in a shoot-out on the beach. Now the lawyer for the construction hut prosecution had learned of Hagen's earlier promiscuity with pistol. 'My lawyer says they're going to tie up the two mistakes – and make me out a mad dog. That's one. Two, I got a date for trial. It's soon. Couple months. That's why I feel I gotta take a coupl'a days off – relax, begin to think myself into condition to deal with this court shit.' Hagen had already told him if it went bad in court, he would be out of the Force. Dolan knew what this would mean to Hagen. It would be a personal disaster.

'That's my news. Here's yours.' Hagen poured himself another glass of the Bruce red, swallowed it down this time as if abandoning any idea that the wine might have finesse, and could now be disposed of as alcohol. 'This guy Stone you had lunch with.'

'D'you know what he wanted?'

'I don't.'

'He wants to buy my old college notes for fifty grand,' Dolan explained. Hagen listened, made no comment. 'You got any idea why some college notes of Leon Markovicz, drowned off Redondo Beach, are of interest? The offer of fifty?'

'Let me tell you about Stone.' Hagen didn't try to answer the question. 'I followed him. After the restaurant.'

Dolan was surprised. 'You were outside Caroldi's? You followed him?'

'Right. He went straight to the airport. He got on a plane to 'Frisco. I got the wire, talked to a pal there who took up on Stone, followed him when he got off the plane.'

'And?'

Hagen was quiet a moment, making up his mind about whether he wanted to be pressed for further information, and how much to hold back. 'This is something else. Congress Springs Pinot Blanc. Know it?' He lifted the second bottle, poured carefully into a fresh glass.

'No.'

'Interesting. Fruit and fine taste of flowers.'

'I've had their Zinfandel. Too oaky.'

'Jesus, you're picky.'

'You had Stone followed off the plane . . .?'

'Let me tell you something else.' Hagen cupped his hand over his nose, tried the aroma as he swirled the liquid in the glass. 'Somebody I can't name told me to see you contacted Stone. I've told you before – when I found your name on our C.R.O. for your grass offences, I had my name programmed in as "contact".'

Dolan knew this, had heard it from Hagen before.

'So your name came up. Someone ran a check on C.R.O. My name came up.'

'Who someone?'

'There has to be discretion now. I have to say I can't tell. Someone important . . .'

Dolan was at sea. 'What the fuck is this, Don?'

Hagen considered. 'I don't know.' He seemed genuinely puzzled. 'Let me go on.' He sipped some more, looked puzzled over the new bottle of wine as well. 'While my pal in 'Frisco P.D. followed Stone, I ran a check on him.'

'Yes?'

'He's "organized crime", John, list of convictions – fraud – six convictions – operates out of 'Vegas. Mistrial on one slap for homicide. He's a bad character. But I believe the deal he's offering you is pukka.'

'Pukka?'

'Right. The guys who asked me to put you on to Stone are genuine, beyond reproach. But Stone is poor news. I think you should be out of the way a few days while I check further.'

'Out of the way?'

'You keep repeating my statements.'

'As questions, because I don't know what you're talking about.'

'I'll spell it out. It's got to be someways worrying that this guy Stone is interested in you. I mean, he's the bad brigade. Now what I want to do is run some further checks before you talk business with him.'

'I thought you were taking days off.'

'Stop crapping. He's heavy. You're a lightweight. I want you to disappear a few days. Hold on to the lecture notes. Keep 'em safe. Something doesn't smell right.'

'Disappear where?'

Hagen told him. 'P.D.'s got a "safe house" – up Arrowhead. I made some enquiries. No one in it. I'll get you in there quietly – say that you're a prospect for a witness on a case. I've been to the safe house. Nice place. Log cabin, wood fires. I'll send you a cook.'

'Cook? What are you talking about?'

'John, do what I tell you. Now finally . . .'

'What?'

'You wouldn't make a detective. I started telling you something. You haven't asked the question. My pal in 'Frisco . . .'

'Followed Stone. Where?'

'That's the question.' Hagen looked gentler and a little bemused. 'He followed Stone from the airport. Stone went to the Russian Consulate and apparently he's spent the night there . . .'

'He did what?'

'He did that . . .'

He got away from Hagen just before lunch. He drove back to Venice, his head lightened by their essays into descriptions of the six-bottle tasting. Dolan checked the rear-view mirror every so often. Russian consulates – Stone a torpedo out of 'Vegas, now coding tiny touches of paranoia into his nerves frayed by the drive up and back from Napa yesterday, a poor night's sleep, and Hagen's incomplete pieces of information.

The breeze was cooling to cold, now coming bone dry out of the Mojave – the first nod and wink from an approaching winter – a day when a million Angelenos would be thinking about their heating and air-conditioning, whether it would survive the next six months. Heating engineers would have a thousand calls before nightfall.

Traffic on Santa Monica heavy enough to make progress slow. Dolan thought he might stop off at a store and get some 'Stouffers' main meals, and something for the sodding dog Mrs Markovicz had bequeathed him. And he wanted some Brie and crackers to go with the Côte Rôtie he'd crack tonight. Tonight he would make tasting notes.

He debated Stone, ex-wife Julie, the Soviet Consulate. Stone in 'organized crime', whatever that meant. None of it made any sense.

And what of Hagen's part in all this? A serving cop about to stand trial, maybe go to jail for shooting an innocent. He'd get off – human life having the value set upon it in Los Angeles. Hagen had left a phone message, 'Go phone Joseph Stone.' Then he'd been very fast on his feet, first following Stone after Caroldi's, then phoning ahead to San Francisco and rustling up the tail. Something mildly sinister to Dolan in the efficiency of Hagen's reactions and actions. Hagen was a fast thinker always, but often a slow mover.

He pulled into the curb outside his mother's house. He went to the porch. An Italian wine merchant in the Valley had been generous. There were two cases of Ricasoli Brolio there. He opened the front door, was about to step in, and recoiled.

There was blood everywhere over the floor in the hall. Some stains reached up two feet to print across the wallpaper. He walked through the hall into the living room, then the kitchen, and back into the dining room. The burglar or burglars had been in a frenzy of hurry. The house had been completely taken apart, first methodically, in the living room, dining room, kitchen area, drawers taken out of cupboards, the contents spread out. Then savagely as the searchers, burglars, whoever they were, ran out of patience at not finding what they wanted, and ran amok. And everywhere blood.

He stood shattered, undecided, in the wrecked hall, then moved upstairs. He would have thought the noise of the demolitions would have brought all Venice running.

On the rug in the middle of the bedroom opposite his lay the huge poodle, in the last pool of its own blood. A long Sabatier chopping knife stuck out of its ribs. The knife had come from a drawer in the kitchen. The dog looked uglier in death than in life. Dolan knelt and touched the corpse. It was still warm.

He went downstairs, surveyed the blitzed room again. There didn't seem to be any point in making a start on it. It would take a day to clean, and he'd have to roll up rugs, carpets. Maybe some of the blood from the stupid dog who had defended his home that wasn't even its own, wouldn't clean up. Parts of or whole walls would have to be repapered.

He phoned Hagen's San Vincente apartment, left a terse description of the visitation on the machine.

He made a brief beginning. Spent half an hour trying to clean the kitchen. Then he sat down to the Côte Rôtie, and without thought or finesse, decanted it and drank. He didn't write any tasting notes.

Dolan sat stiff and regretting on the solid wooden kitchen chair. He had finished the Côte Rôtie, and then opened and finished another one, wondering what to do, but knowing that he would have to wait for Hagen to phone.

Hagen phoned at three. His drawl seemed edged

with more than a hint of worry. 'I want to discuss with you.'

'Where?'

'On the phone. I'm in North Los Angeles. On a stake. I can't leave.'

Dolan could hear sounds of traffic down the line.

'Any idea who hit you? What's missing? The lecture notes?'

'No, I had them in the car.'

'May have nothing to do with Stone, or anything. May have just been a hit.'

'I haven't been burglarized in six years.'

'Maybe.' Hagen took his time – working out something. 'I don't get this.'

'I don't get it either.'

'Well,' a hesitation from the detective, then, 'John, you're too good a fund of free booze and clean wisdom. You may be getting into something over your head. What I said about the "safe house" in Arrowhead. Go there. Here's the address.' There was a moment's pause. 'One-one-two-three Pine Acre Heights, Arrowhead. Go there.'

'Now?'

'I'll phone you later.'

'Wait,' Dolan said sharply. Hagen had a habit of putting down the receiver on people as soon as he considered his part of the call was over. 'Look. Stone, a burglary, a dead dog, "organized crime". Leon's lecture notes. And you. I want you to make some sense of it – or I don't take any more advice from you or anybody.'

'I hear you.' Hagen put down the phone.

Dolan found a large black plastic dirt sack, went up to the bedroom, manoeuvred the Sabatier knife out of the stiffening dog, put the corpse in the bag, took it downstairs and back to the yard – stuck it in a waste bin. The corpse occupied the whole of the waste bin.

He went back into the house, and out, remembering he'd forgotten to check the mail box this morning. Three wine lists and a letter. The letter was from Mrs Markovicz. He stood in the bloodstained hall and read it.

'Dear John Dolan. Millions are starving all over the world. It's a conspiracy of those who believe in "Super Race". Leon knew this, tried to stop them. They are following me. They are trying to destroy me, because I was a part of him. You and only you can save me from peril. Ring 204–5604. Greta.'

He rang the number and hung on and on. There was no answer. He phoned Hagen's answering machine. 'Don, I got mail this morning. Letter from Mrs Markovicz. I'll read it.' He read the letter into the recorder. Then he added, 'Can you check that phone number? I'm on my way to Arrowhead.'

He went upstairs, packed a soft case. In locking up the house he found the rear wash-room window that the burglars had forced.

He headed out.

The day was warmer. Almost without being able to help himself, his spirits lifted as he left the jaded city. Traffic was light for the hour as he headed north and east. Then he hit the hills. So much oxygen up here, so many trees, as if this was a last redoubt of the nature that had been driven back, beaten, and nearly defeated, but had brought in new reserves to wait for a counter-attack on man below.

The traffic slowed as motorists gawked at the scenery. The lake showed, shrouded in mist running down from the fir-lined roads. The air grew colder but gentler, screened from the hill-top breezes by the windbreaks of trees. He felt calmer now. Hagen would get some answers together. Meanwhile he'd let most of the worries roll over him and down the long routes back to Los Angeles.

He found the log cabin, drove up a path which petered out thirty yards from its door, got out of the Chrysler, stood, flexed his muscles stiffened in the hour and a half drive. He went to the door, tried it. It was locked. He rang the bell.

The door opened and a girl stood there.

'John Dolan?'

'Yes.' He felt awkward, as a slight pause grew while she scrutinized him.

'Come in,' she said.

'Who are you?'

'I'm your cook.'

She walked ahead of him down a pine-walled hallway into a room with a large window view of trees climbing a slope beyond. She turned by a bookcase, smiled. 'Christa. I was about to make some China tea. D'you like China tea?'

'Yes.' He followed her into a little kitchen. 'A cook for the police department. What kind of life is that?'

'I have to leave a message you've arrived.' She went to the wall phone and dialled. Dolan studied her as she combed the fingers of one hand through her long auburn hair. He was aware of looking at her, an unbelieving look, and almost crudely ticking off some list of her physical attributes as if to lock into some clue of who she was and why she was there.

She was about five feet six, age twenty-three to twenty-five, blue eyes, oval face, no distinguishing marks. But then he rethought the description. In fact, the face and body did have a distinguishing mark: she was very good-looking indeed. A perfectly made body, great legs, intelligent face with good bone structure, clear skin, and nice colour on her cheeks. She would be nearer twenty-five than twenty-three. She was well dressed, the clothes casual but obviously expensive – dark green boiler suit, and cashmere V-neck in brown-and-green check. Gold Piaget wrist-watch, familiar to Dolan because he'd once had a girlfriend who'd valued her Piaget more than her life.

'Detective Hagen, please.' There was a pause, then she was talking to Hagen. 'It's me. He's here.'

She held out the phone for Dolan. He took it from her. 'Don, I've met the cook.'

'Yeah, yeah,' Hagen said vaguely, as if he'd been interrupted in the middle of something important, and this was not important. 'Hold on.' A phone was ringing at his end of the line. He picked it up and shouted a couple of 'yes's and 'no's into it and banged it down. Then he was back on Dolan's line. 'What about her?'

Christa was saying, 'I'll get my cigarettes.'

'Okay.'

She left the kitchen.

He questioned Hagen. 'All right, who is she?'

'She's a cook.' Hagen hesitated. 'Don't let her get too ambitious. Steaks, fresh vegetables, maybe a reheat job on Sarah Lee. Her coffee's lousy, I'm told. Don't drink her coffee.'

'Hold it,' Dolan said loudly, anticipating that Hagen was about to put down the phone. 'What are you up to? Who is this girl?'

'Listen, I checked the phone number, the Mrs Markovicz note you got. It's a bungalow in the Sears Mount Motel. She's gone. Stayed the night and checked out. Speak to you later.'

'Don,' Dolan tried again. 'Who is this girl?'

'She's a great looking broad and you have to relax.'

'What does that mean – I have to relax?'

There was a pause on the other end of the line and then a grating noise that lasted five seconds. It was Hagen laughing. 'She's nice and respectable. You need a lay. My feeling is you won't get to base. Who knows? Meanwhile she talks, she cooks. Now fuck off, I'm working on your case.' He put the phone down.

Christa walked back in as Dolan replaced the receiver. She stood and looked at him as she lit her cigarette.

'I owe you an apology,' he said.

'Why?'

He didn't know, just felt that their introduction had gone amiss. 'I was expecting a fat lady with apron and rolling pin.'

'You disappointed?'

'No.'

She smiled, and it was a nice smile. He decided that this was a cool and sophisticated girl, warm under the surface. He liked a girl with some reserve. Equally he liked a little humour.

'Don and I are good friends,' she said. The voice was nice too, deep and softly accented. 'I phoned him earlier. He said a pal would be out here and he'd just realized you might not be able to cook.'

She made the tea, organized a tray and cups, took it into the living room, and put it down on a table by the window that overlooked the rising hill of trees.

'Have you known Don long?' he asked her.

'Some time.'

'Childhood friends?'

'Flattery.' She smiled.

'The meal you're to cook, is it dinner tonight?'

'Right.' She poured the tea.

'What do we do in a Los Angeles Police Department safe house between now and dinner?'

'I'd like to walk – if that's compatible with your security.'

'I don't think there's any threat to me.'

'Don thinks so.'

'What does he say?'

'Well, he hasn't said much. Never does. But aren't "safe houses" for people like threatened witnesses?'

'I'm not a threatened witness.'

She sipped her tea. 'I always thought that Arrowhead was a Disneyworld showcase constructed for the tourist. In fact it's very beautiful.'

He watched her. She obviously had another talent, the instant capacity to relax – he liked that in a girl – the ability to arrive in a strange house, take off her shoes, and curl up in a chair.

'What d'you do when you're not in your kitchens?'

The blue eyes came round on him. 'What kind of answer would you like?'

'D'you work? Do you have a career?'

'A long time ago and in another world, I was trying to be an actress. Now I'm recently divorced. That's a career.'

The actress bit added up. Her make-up, the way she carried herself. 'Me, a year,' Dolan said.

'You, a year, what?'

'Divorced a year.'

'That's one poignant topic for discussion over dinner.'

'Right.'

Now she was studying him, weighing him up and adding her own calculations. 'What about you? I like mystery. Don says he doesn't know how you make a living.'

'Don knows well how I make a living. And I'm surprised he didn't tell you. He tells everyone.'

'All right, he told me.'

'Told you what?'

'That you write a wine column for *Village West*. They don't pay you much. But you phone up wine stores, importers – say you're going to write about their wine. And they send you cases of it. And you sell the cases. Yes?'

'Yes.'

'Who d'you sell the cases to?'

'Reuben's Wine Store, Encino.'

'What's the scam worth, kid?' She said it Humphrey-Bogart-style, out of the corner of her mouth.

'Average a grand a month.'

'You're joking.' She was surprised.

'Nope.'

'Don says you're more "con" than "artist",'

'Nope. According to a guy called Stone, I'm a "good man". That's what he says.'

She went quiet a moment, looking at him, debating something with herself. 'What are the chances that someone will walk in with a gun and blow your brains out?'

'Jesus,' Dolan said.

'Are you a stool pigeon for some Senate crime investigation?'

'I don't know why Don asked me to come here.'

'I see.' She spoke softly, almost inaudibly, but he realized that she was disguising something, and it was excitement. That intrigued him. First, because danger never turned him on. The second reason was more an interrogative – did this good-looking girl just get her imagination stimulated by this stake-out, or was anything else turned on?

'Are we going to walk?'

'Fine,' she said. She finished her tea. 'Let's go to a market. There's nothing in the house.'

They set off. He had to get a crumpled raincoat out of the back seat of the Chrysler. There was an edge to the air up here, a darkness among the trees. She set off long-strided while he locked the car doors. He had to move fast to catch up with her.

'Let's say somebody starts shooting at you. What will you do?'

'Panic first. Then I run.'

'What about me?'

'My advice is don't count on me.'

'Okay.' And her long stride increased. Then she decided something. 'I don't think you're the kind that gets killed.'

'Why?'

'You're like Don. As soon as I saw you, I thought, Don likes you because you're a certain type.'

'What certain type?'

'He's a winner. A definition of a winner is sometimes a person who succeeds because they make others around them lose.'

'That sounds like a ten-hour discussion. How long have we got?'

She told him. She said she could stay until eleven that night, and explained that a cab was going to call for her. It was obvious she was laying out the conditions of the visit. And he could understand that she'd want to make it clear that he mustn't draw wrong conclusions. She was just a friend of Hagen's who'd been intrigued enough to meet him. That, on the surface, would be all.

They ended up in a supermarket in Blue Lake. She got the idea that they would buy things that had to do with England – English marmalade, English Worcestershire sauce, English muffins, and English roast beef for the main course.

They were loaded with shopping when they set off back for the cabin.

'What about you?'

'What about me?'

'Where d'you come from?'

'Country girl. Born and raised in Toilet, Virginia, population one hundred ninety-two . . .'

'And what about your husband?'

'My ex-husband is forty. Works for the Grace

Masson Corporation. He's an executive V-P. There's nothing else to say about him.'

'Where do you live?'

'Place in L.A. with a girlfriend. You must come visit.' She was obviously making a point of steering him away from talk of her. He wondered why.

'Is Don a close friend?'

'He turns up from time to time.'

'You sound sad about it.'

'Saddest thing I've ever known.' Then she gave a little smile.

They got back to the cabin and ferried the four bags of groceries round to the kitchen door.

In the kitchen she headed over to the wall phone. 'I have to make a call to a girlfriend, find out how to cook this beef.'

'I know,' he said. 'Half an hour a pound in a two-seventy-five oven.' He took out the wrapped beef and looked at the printed weight. 'Two and a half pounds. A little over an hour.'

'How d'you know that?'

'I always was a bachelor. Even during my marriage. Then I was a bachelor cooking for two.'

'That's a pity.'

'No. It was fine.'

'If it's going to take an hour, we could walk again?'

They walked in the long shadows of dark trees through the sharp air, down, following tiny roads, to within a dozen yards of the lake. A couple of times they took shortcuts over dripping embankments and Dolan helped her with a hand, and finally they ended up hand in hand. At one point they were passing a private driveway. Suddenly they were confronted by a huge dog that moved in on them barking hysterically. Dolan was reminded of that late and not lamented Markovicz dog. 'Watch this,' he shouted to her. 'Dogs are all lousy bluffers . . .' He put on a manic expression and slowly moved in on the dog. The huge dog moved in on him with some awesome growling until he was within five feet of it, and then suddenly it turned and fled.

He laughed with her laughter.

They got back to the cabin and he built a fire.

The meat cooked. They made the vegetables together. It was nearly seven o'clock. They ate leisurely. He found himself talking easily, a role that was unfamiliar to him on a first meeting. She seemed to draw out confidence. There was no guilt there. She seemed genuinely interested in him. That surprised and pleased him. Then it was eight-thirty and they were on brandies.

A decision, more an impulse, and he got up and moved close to her where she sat on the couch. She was looking at him undecided.

He felt he could put it straight. 'Why go back tonight? Stay with me. Sleep with me.'

Her eyes were cold, but thoughtful. And then her expression slowly altered. She gave a little shrug. But he realized she'd made up her mind, reached an unspoken agreement with him.

Night settled black over the trees. No stars, and no streetlights visible from the front bedroom of the cabin eyrie. The wind rising to rustle the trees and bang the screens on the outside doors. He relaxed into a feeling of security and inviolability.

He couldn't remember anyone quite as good as her in bed. There was a girl he'd known years ago who was a faint echo. He had assumed the mores had changed. He had assumed that the ambivalence of the sex act of his marriage – was he balling his wife, or was she simply screwing herself on him? – was the modern way. Now in the cabin, near a lake, through a long haul of their lovemaking, he remembered that this was how it could be, not the cold comfort of nights between the thighs of his wife, but something generous, and packaged like an expensive gift, and given.

She had been sitting on him, straddling him, arcing her body back and forth. Now she slowly came down on his chest, complete within seconds of the earthquake that shook his limbs. He turned her aside and cradled her head in his arms, then lay there, content, contemplating disparate thoughts. The cabin ceiling, the pattern of its paper, the girl, her lovely body, the possibilities of a serious involvement,

'What are you thinking?' Her voice was dry and low, difficult to understand.

'Nothing. Nothing important.' He had been aware that her eyes, still dewy and moist, had been studying him in the half light from the open door to the hall.

'Bastard,' she said gently. 'When I decided to come here, I promised myself, whatever happened, I wouldn't end up in bed with some Don Hagen nominee.'

He couldn't think of an adequate answer. He was quiet a moment. 'Listen,' he said eventually. 'Be honest with me. Your coming here, right? You're not part of some weird scheme of Don's to check me out? You are who you say you are?'

'I don't know what you mean by "some scheme". But what I've said about me is the truth.'

He decided he couldn't see any reason why it shouldn't be.

'Hey you,' she said. 'Again.'

'Shortly.'

Her right hand moved slowly down between his legs. 'How long does it take to recover?'

He looked at her. 'Half an hour. I bet you can't do anything about that.'

He lost his bet.

Then it was ten o'clock. He'd been unaware of the passage of hours.

'I have a cab to catch,' she said.

'Come on. Don't leave now.' The room was cold, and their bed warm and snug. He'd require a great deal of resolution to get up.

'I told you. Okay?' Her voice firm. He knew she meant it.

They got up and got dressed. The cab came twenty minutes later. As they walked down to it she turned and kissed him briefly on the cheek.

'I'll see you tomorrow?'

'We'll see,' he said.

'Wait a minute. You're cook.'

'You're a better cook than me.' She said it matter-of-factly, distanced, as if some casual meeting was over, and hadn't added to much.

'How do I contact you?' He didn't want to be too eager or alarmed. 'Your phone number . . .'

'Don's got it,' she said. She stepped into the cab and it drove off.

Feeling put down he turned round and headed back to the house. The phone started ringing.

'Yeah?' He spoke into the receiver.

'How goes it?' It was Hagen.

'Good,' he said flatly.

'Where's the girl?'

'Christa? She's gone home.'

'Right. I've some more information for you. Stone was followed from the Russian Consulate to First City Bank. He checked out a hundred and fifty grand in cash. Maybe you're going to be rich.'

'Maybe fifty grand for me, fifty for Julie.'

'And the third fifty?'

'Third fifty?'

'Who else was in your class taking Markovicz' notes?'

'That's a very good question.'

'Answer it.'

'There were others, but there was a guy called Colville who stayed the course.'

'Explain.'

Dolan tried. There were maybe ten or a dozen signed up for the root stock and hybridization study course. Two or three lectures in and Markovicz had started to cry as he worked at the blackboard. Five lectures in and he had only three students left. Himself, Julie and a bright guy, Dennis Colville, who already had a degree from somewhere or other and was now studying his first year of agriculture. His father – like Dolan's – had a farm. Julie and he had stayed with Markovicz because they pitied him, never understood what he was at, but had an instinct that they were in the presence of a genius who happened to be a human being destroying himself.

'So this Dennis Colville stayed the course?'

'Right.'

'What happened to him?' Hagen said.

'At year end he gave up on agriculture, went on to a Rand Think Tank, in some minor capacity,' Dolan offered. 'A shit, but a clever shit.'

'Did he understand what Markovicz was talking about?'

'Maybe. Could be.'

'I'll see if I can find him.'

'What are you up to?. What exactly are you doing?'

Hagen laughed openly. 'It's okay. I'm looking after you.' He replaced the phone.

He phoned back an hour later just as Dolan was thinking of bed and sleeping off his sexual activity, a large meal, wine and brandy.

'Colville's not at Rand.'

'He's not?'

'You gotta way that everything I tell you becomes a

question. He's not at Rand. They say he's at M.I.T. Department of Biological Sciences.'

'Where Markovicz originated.' For no reason he could explain, Dolan felt a little inner reaction of unease, disquiet.

'Is that right?'

'What's he doing there?'

'I don't know.'

'How long d'you think I'm going to stay up here?'

'How long?' Hagen asked the question back. 'Stone's going to contact you, leave a message on your answer machine. I want to be around, surveillancing you, if he comes to buy.'

Dolan said nothing.

'Deal?'

'Maybe.'

'Relax a few days.'

'Why?'

'Too many questions, John Dolan. Let it roll over you. You're in good hands.'

'If you're playing it straight.'

Hagen laughed. 'You better believe it.' He put down the phone.

Dolan made black coffee, drank two cups fast to try to chase the last of the alcohol out of his bloodstream. He debated, hesitated as he walked aimlessly round the ground floor of the cabin. Then he made up his mind. He packed the suitcase, went out to the car, and started driving back through the night to Los Angeles.

There were two messages on the answer machine. The first, almost incomprehensible, was from Mrs Markovicz. She was drunk. She said a cassette was on the way. Hitler's Storm Troops were out to get her. There was a cassette in the mail. She didn't leave an address or phone number.

The second was from Stone. 'Dolan, I'm ready to do business. It's twenty after eleven. I'll contact eight a.m. Have the merchandise ready.' Stone's voice sounded tired and strained.

Dolan looked in the mail box. In it was a brown packet, postmarked Napa, and containing a Sony video cassette. There was no note with the cassette. Also in the mail, a cheque from Reuben's Wine Store in the Valley. Two thousand dollars. His finances, for a change, were beginning to look reasonable. He debated. He could afford to invest in an air fare. And the dog's blood had now dried to brown and was somehow even more offensive – it resembled smeared faeces on the walls and floors. So he wanted to get out of the house. And M.I.T. looked like a candidate for some enquiries. Colville was at M.I.T. Markovicz had been evicted from M.I.T., and what were the real reasons? Dolan went to sleep in the kitchen chair.

He'd set the alarm and woke with it at six in the morning. He phoned 'Information'. 'Could I have a number for the Dean's Office, Department of Biological Sciences, M.I.T.?'

It would be just after nine in Boston. The Dean's secretary was already at her desk.

He told her he was science correspondent for *Village West*. He'd be in Boston later today. Was there any chance that he could talk to the Dean about Professor Leon Markovicz recently drowned off Redondo Beach? She said it was unlikely that the Dean could make himself available at such short notice but she would speak to him, and then phone Dolan back.

The return call came fifteen minutes later. Yes, Dean Gower could see him for half an hour around five.

He drove to the airport.

There was a query about his signature on the Diner's Club cheque for his ticket, and a delay of ten minutes. He was asked to sign another blank. This time the signature satisfied. He realized the strain of the last two days was beginning to put a shake in his hand.

Dolan arrived in Boston in a storm. The plane had made good time from L.A. and was twenty minutes early. The appointment with Gower at the Institute was scheduled an hour hence, and the journey would take half an hour. The air was cold. The wind cut through his battered Missoni on the uncovered ten-yard walk from the plane into the terminal building.

He walked down the lanes of Pirelli flooring to the arrivals area and paused. Few people around. He looked for some direction to take, saw a bank of seats facing the picture windows of the concourse with a view over the runways. He moved towards them.

They were lined up like theatre seats to view the falling sheets of rain. He sat and looked out at the storm, decided the pause might well be a convenience, a chance to gather his wits before confronting the Dean. He sensed something not quite right. The verbose secretary had been sure the Dean would be too busy at such short notice to see him. 'I will consult with the Dean and refer to his schedule of engagements, and if the Dean is agreeable, I will return your call with the offer of an appointment but at a time to suit convenience. I must point out that he is an extremely busy man.' Dolan watched the rain and puzzled on it. His mind went back to the last time he had been in this airport. Six years ago. He'd been passing through on an interchange from Montreal to Houston. He'd met his father. A rare meeting. The two would perhaps manage one or two quietly muttered meetings a year. His father was in Boston for a farmer's convention – an annual reminder as he dolefully trooped the corridors of some blank hotel filled with babbling farmers, that he was a failure – that he'd never got enough land together to make it work. A failure in the final stages. A useless army career followed by a pointless farming one. Because he had no money he always made a fuss about taking his son out to a restaurant, paying for his meal, with 'French wine. You choose it, son. You know so much about it. But I usually find the house wine in a restaurant like this perfectly good.' A caution there for Dolan not to order anything but the house wine. The last meeting at Boston Airport, in the old building that had been replaced by this rain-soaked glasshouse, had found the old guy speechless. Unable to take his son to a restaurant, unable to say anything about the farmer's convention, unable to discuss anything about himself, and Dolan's mother's alcoholism. The old man had become tongue-tied. And Dolan had been caught out by his father's sudden hopeless silence. The meeting left a sour taste which he now savoured again as he studied the washed runways and taxiing planes.

He got up. He'd take a cab and arrive early at the Dean's office and sit it out.

He'd been to Harvard ten years before, to visit some girlfriend's brother, a prick, in the law school. The drive from Logan International up and round to Cambridge and on to fork to Harvard or M.I.T. was through another country.

Cambridge looked a different town, higher, with dense new buildings, longer in spread. A sense of urgency about it. A place on the move, not like the towns of L.A., retired into materialistic exhaustion. There was enough new glass and freeway and activity for the subconscious to be asking, 'What goes on here?' It all seemed measured, organized. The people on the sidewalk, cocooned in rainwear, purposeful in gait. The punctuation of sections of old town, low brickwork still stained from coal burning decades ago, only served to emphasize the new brashness and bravery of a place, moving with selected parts of another America towards economic recovery after years of doldrums.

The cab driver negotiated the dozens of peremptory direction signs, leaned back in his private half of a brand new Chevrolet, steering with one index finger, and was silent.

Dolan had not visited M.I.T. before. A factory city, he decided, but the production lines designed in granite and Doric columns, or low level tombstone shapes of Bauhaus glass and steel. There were not enough trees, he decided. And the lawns so much like Astroturf, the effect must be deliberate, an aseptic background that would not intimidate the minds of pure science into thoughts of impractical aesthetics. Unfriendly, he decided.

The Department of Biological Sciences rolled down from a small hill into some unforeseen conclusion in a valley of grey cement beyond. The Dean's building was new and aggressive. A low block badly out of scale with some airport hangar high-roofed buildings around it. But the marbled entrance hall and the leather-walled elevators placed the design as successful, if the effect was to promote an atmosphere of the gentleman's club at the top end of the market.

The secretary had babbled an acceptance of early delivery of the visitor, to the two porters on desk duty. Dolan went to the fourth floor. She was waiting by the elevator to guide him through a fifty-yard tour of soft blue carpet to the Dean's office. She was a small woman in her mid-fifties. A demented ex-Bell telephone operator – Dolan decided.

'Traffic irregularity does concern our visitors and we find many arrive late, and so we're obliged that you are certainly on time. Though it would be remiss of one to suggest that the Dean is immediately available to respond. May I enquire if you would care for a coffee or a soda while you wait?'

'Coffee. Regular.'

The coffee came from a machine which had also mixed into the cup a quantity of stale tea. He sipped the liquid and let her talk, which she was able to do while typing into a word processor. 'It's a problem area to explain to some who wish access to Dean Gower that three months to accrue an exact comprehension of faculty works and affairs in order to take rein, is no long time.'

'I'm sorry?'

'Dean Gower has been in his post three months and has a lot of catching up to do. I think I'm apologizing – you've arrived early, he may be late.'

'Don't worry. You know – no plans.'

'You'll oblige us by your patience if the Dean is delayed.'

'So he's only been three months in the job?'

'He replaced Dean Corly with whom I had the pleasure of fifteen years' association, as personal private secretary.'

'What happened to Dean Corly?'

'He retired . . . he required himself to pay more time to his family.'

'I may have made a miscalculation here. For no good reason I assumed Dean Gower would know the late Professor Markovicz.'

'I put your request to Dean Gower and his reponse was positive that he would see you. If he did not know Professor Markovicz, and felt he would not be of any use to you, he would have offered that an interview would not be of relevance. Don't concern yourself that you might be at cross purposes. He turns down certain requests for meetings. Yours he has not.'

'Did he know Leon Markovicz?'

'I'm not sure.'

'There are some weird stories about him.' Dolan wanted to draw the lady out – maybe he'd learn more from her babble than anyone.

But her expression went colder, as if she'd gauged the calculation. 'I'm not familiar with any stories about Professor Markovicz.' Her attention now went fully back to the word processor. He persevered with the tea-coffee mix. Half an hour passed before the intercom buzzed on her desk. She answered it, took her time replacing the phone and then looked up at him. 'The Dean will see you now.' She indicated one of the two large oak doors behind her. Dolan got up.

A man stood in the long oak-panelled room. In the dozen seconds since the intercom had buzzed he'd already picked up another phone and was now speaking quietly into it. He stood in front of an impressively large desk. It was covered in black leather to match the three easy chairs in the room. The man nodded and gestured to Dolan. Dolan sat in a deep armchair and studied Dean Gower.

He was medium height, broad-shouldered, thin face, white hair immaculate as if fresh from a barber's hands. He had an expensive suit, white silk shirt, club tie, hand-made shoes. Large gold and lapis lazuli cufflinks peeked out of double cuffs. A man, thought Dolan, who takes at least an hour to dress every morning. He looked like a movie star on the set of a Hollywood soap opera about big business. The phone call, which consisted of monosyllables and half sentences, ended. Dean

Gower came across, sat down, and looked at Dolan closely for the first time. The look, Dolan decided, began well, before deteriorating into criticism and a slight downturn of the corner of the mouth.

'I'm Gower.'

'John Dolan.'

'*Village West*?' The Dean got straight to the point. Having decided on the insubstantiality of Dolan's appearance, his next move would be to some exchange of enough lightweight information to get rid of him. 'I've not heard of *Village West*.'

'Circulation two-hundred-and-forty thousand, all metropolitan L.A. Any Los Angeleno would know us.' Dolan kept his voice bright and unintimidated.

'So you have some questions about Leon Markovicz?'

'Yes.'

'They are?' The Dean had taken the decision to abandon any politesse.

'I met him when I was a student at Davis.'

'Yes?'

'I got to know him. Not closely. But we spent time together, in and out of class.'

'Yes?'

'I'm interested in his story.'

'What story?'

Dolan parried the rudeness with a little shrug. 'I understand that he had a genuinely innovative mind. That he was a maverick. But that he was greatly respected. I'm interested in what he was working on when he died – committed suicide.'

'And what was he working on? I know you're supposed to be asking the questions, Mr Dolan, but I'm unclear . . .'

'He was a biologist. He was into plant genetics. He was important enough in his field to have worked here. That work must have been known to his colleagues. I wondered if you could tell me anything about it, past or present. Evidently his past work is interesting enough folk that they're running around his old students like myself, trying to acquire his lecture notes.'

There was a silence. Then Gower spoke, his voice lower. 'What can I tell you? I came to this post some three months back. Of course I've been associated with the Institute for some time. I never met Markovicz. I was aware of his work.'

'I want to know why he left here.'

'Well, you get hearsay around the place which I cannot confirm or deny. However, the man is dead. The hearsay is that there were some missing laboratory materials. Expensive materials. Unaccounted for.'

'Can you say more than that?'

'I can't. All I know is there was an auditor's report and expensive laboratory materials had disappeared.'

'I see.'

'Then there was his extremely erratic behaviour with faculty students. Emotionally erratic.'

'So he was asked to leave?'

'Yes. He was a fine scientist. But his behaviour was eccentric in the extreme. This Institute has standards which no one may trespass.'

'Yet he went on to get a job at Davis.'

'He had friends and admirers. I think it was through their offices. We have a reputation. Davis is not a leading institution. Apparently he was very difficult to deal with at Davis.'

'We had a hint of that,' Dolan offered, trying to make the conversation a collaboration to draw the man out. 'He was a lonely, nervous man. On occasions we saw . . . well, he was obviously a disturbed man . . .'

Gower said nothing.

'There was also the odd behaviour of his wife.'

'Quite. Now, what you're telling me I know, what do you think I can tell you?'

'Why d'you think somebody would go the rounds of people like myself, trying to buy up Leon Markovicz' lecture notes?'

'Perhaps what he was working on has some industrial application. Perhaps some large business corporation with money to spend on research is interested in his work. Perhaps he was on to something with important commercial applications.'

'I had thought of the commercial angle, Dean Gower. There is another angle.'

'Yes?'

'Supposing some of his work, ideas, calculations, were indeed in his students' notes, and supposing someone or some organization wanted to suppress his work, that would also be a reason to try and acquire the students' notes, in order to destroy them.'

There was an imperceptible shift in the Dean's eyes. A pause, and then, 'I don't really understand. Why would anybody suppress, want to suppress, Leon's work?'

'That's a possible question I'm trying to answer.'

The phone rang. The Dean got up with an irritated look and paced to his desk. He picked up the phone. 'I wasn't to be disturbed,' he said sharply into it. There was a pause. He turned to Dolan. 'I'm extremely sorry. I have a very important call to take. Could you leave me for one moment?'

It wasn't couched as a request.

'Yes of course.' Dolan got up, walked to the door and out.

He sat outside, looking at the secretary now buried in concentration at the word processor. Five minutes later Dean Gower appeared.

'Mr Dolan. Apologies. But something's come up. I have to attend to it immediately. Please leave your telephone number. The board views importantly our relations with the press. I'm going to find, you'll have to give me a day or two, someone in the faculty who knew Leon best, and ask them to contact you.'

'There is someone here. Dennis Colville.'

'Colville.' The Dean took a moment considering the name. 'He's recently joined the department. I must now attend to some matters with my secretary.'

It was the brush-off, and the brick wall, and the handshake, and Dolan knew it.

He left the Dean's office and went down to the porters. They were helpful. They found a phone number for Colville in Chelsea and Dolan offered a five-dollar bill, and they phoned there, and the lab, and paged the canteen, and the Resident's office, but Colville had not been seen for a week. They called a cab to take him back to the airport.

In the cab he considered. It was the shift in the Dean's eyes when he'd mentioned suppression of Markovicz' work. That shift, and the haste to get the interview over coupled with the fact that the Dean had offered him, a no one, an interview at such short notice in the first place. Everything stunk. It hadn't been a wasted trip.

He got back to L.A. around nine. There were another two messages from Stone on the tape, plus a few blank starts which he took to be other Stone attempts to check again with the number. Christa had called, and Hagen.

He called Stone.

'Jesus, Dolan, where have you been?'

'I travel a lot.'

'I got money here for you. Cash. I'll be over.'

'Tomorrow. Say noon. I have to be up early.'

'I want to see you tonight!' There was an urgency close to desperation in Stone's voice.

'I'm just going out. Noon tomorrow.'

'You have definitely got the notes?'

'I told you.' Dolan replaced the phone, made a mental note to set the alarm for eight. He could get the notebooks xeroxed between ten and noon, ready to hand over the originals to Stone.

He phoned D.B.'s. Karen answered.

'Listen, this is not late at night, for you. I want to come over. I want to use D.B.'s video. I've got a tape I have to see.'

'There's people here,' Karen said, not pleased. 'I don't know if they're coming or going. I'll ask D.B.'

'Your video's in the bedroom. I can sit quiet.'

'I think there are some people in the bedroom. Dolan, D.B.'s got new friends. The place is like a bordello.'

'Karen, may I come over?' He put it as a blunt question.

''Course.'

He phoned Christa.

She answered immediately, almost as if she was poised waiting by the phone. 'Hagen's been looking for you. You're a bad boy.'

'I'm a "good man". Stone says so.'

'You in Lake Arrowhead?'

'No.'

'Why not?'

'I'm not.'

'Where are you?'

'I'd like to see you. Can I come in an hour?'

'That'll be near midnight.'

'Is that a time check or turn down?'

'Come over.'

'I haven't eaten. Have you got any food? You're my cook.'

'I'll find something.'

It took twenty minutes to drive to D.B.'s house.

D.B. had got rid of his guests. A blanket of marijuana smoke, and Karen, greeted him. 'D.B.'s upstairs. He's tired. Don't start him drinking.'

'Okay.'

They went up to the bedroom. D.B. was already in bed, half asleep. He came awake. 'We had a football team here, and camp followers.'

'I know.'

'How d'you know?'

'The house is wrecked.'

'Is it?' D.B. asked Karen.

'No. It's a mess.'

'They break anything?'

'No, but they smoked all your grass.' Karen didn't seem too displeased about it.

'You got a tape. Know how to play it?' he asked Dolan.

'Yes.'

The tape lasted four minutes. It consisted of some camera work of microscope slides, and then two minutes of Markovicz juggling. The cheap video camera, or the poor lighting, made the opening section difficult to decipher.

'What are they?' D.B. asked.

'They're plant cells,' Dolan said. He didn't want D.B. to talk while he concentrated on the pictures.

'What does that mean? "Silent Soldier"?' Karen asked.

'I don't know.' Dolan himself was wondering what the lettering on the bottom of each of the dozen slides meant. Each slide had the words 'Silent Soldier', and a three digit reference number. 'I've never heard of "Silent Soldier".'

After the two minutes of the microscope slides came the juggling sequence.

The setting seemed to be the ocean. To the left of frame, the edge of the grey truck Dolan had last seen at Hunt's place in Napa.

There was sound accompanying this section of the tape. Not a lot of it. The quiet drumming of a generator inside the truck, and the faint splash of waves on the beach. The tape finished. D.B. should have been in with some comment, but said nothing.

'May I play it again?' Dolan asked.

'Go ahead.'

Dolan rewound it, started the poor quality pictures again.

There was silence in the room when the slide photos ended and the juggling started, and now detectable on the sound track, the intakes of Markovicz' breath as he stooped his large frame and pulled the green rubber balls from his pockets, lining them into the ellipse of rising and falling. At the end he had seven balls in the air.

'Who is he?' Karen had moved nearer to the TV set.

'A old lecturer of mine. He's the guy I mentioned, drowned off Redondo Beach.'

'Look at his face.' Karen was nodding her head towards the set.

'How would you describe the expression in his eyes?'

'He looks frightened.'

'You got it.'

'Got what?'

Dolan didn't know. 'An old man juggling balls is frightened . . . Why?'

Karen was silent a moment. Finally she said, 'It's like a metaphor for something . . .'

'Metaphor?'

'Well, the moving green balls, they're not unlike the cells, the circular plant cells, on the first part of the tape. You say he's a biologist. Don't biologists now juggle with cells?'

Dolan felt his heart miss a beat. He was looking staggered at Karen. He was trying to work out some reason, any reason, for not thinking that she had hit on it.

He had Christa's directions but it was not easy to find the house, somewhere back of Laurel Canyon, where architects had penned structures directly on to hillsides, blind in both eyes to the knowledge that, come the big shake, they would all be changing their addresses to Sunset Boulevard.

He followed her into the grey mirrored hall of the apartment. 'Quite a place,' he said, as soon as he saw the main room.

'The girl I share with is a leading decorator,' Christa said.

He was studying the layout. It had the simplicity and elegance of dark woods, chrome and polished leather. It didn't necessarily add up to a great deal of money being spent. The ground floor was one open cool space, as wide as the full frontage of the mission-style house, but going back about thirty feet. The lighting in the room was as subdued as a brown-out, and at first glance it was difficult to fathom where it came from. Along the glass and steel tables and polished wood surfaces were *objets virtus*, and gold-framed pictures of Christa at various stages in her development from babe, to jail bait, to mature home-breaker. The last photo placed her about twenty. He turned and saw almost the identical expression on the real thing.

She took both his hands gently in her soft fingers. 'So, midnight lunch?' she said quietly. 'Hungry?'

'What have you got?'

'Steaks.'

'Put the steak in a sandwich. Does this place have a bedroom?'

'Take the steps. You'll find a room with a big bed.'

'Can I help you?'

'No.'

Five minutes later she climbed the narrow stairs and headed into the main bedroom. He was sitting on the end of the bed.

She put the tray, the two steak sandwiches, a salad, and a bottle of red wine, down on a low table.

'What did you do today?' he asked.

'Where have you been?' she countered.

'Business. I bought fifty million shares of I.B.M. What did you do?'

'Nothing much. Talked to my ex-husband. Never a terrific experience.' She moved the low table round so that he could reach the tray. She joined him, sitting on the bed.

'I thought you said your husband was nice enough.'

'Not when he talks about his psychiatric problems. People don't have a right to mental equilibrium, they have to earn it. Actually, it makes me depressed to talk about him.'

'Don't.'

'Let's talk about us.' Her expression became more serious. 'When I went up to Arrowhead yesterday, as I told you, I had no intention of ending up in bed with you. That's the truth. But you screwed that. However, there's a problem. Obviously I'm a single girl with a lovely personality and it happens I've got another relationship going.'

'Okay,' he said quietly.

'But let me sort that out. For however long you're alive and interested, I'd like to check with you.'

'Fine.'

'All I'm saying is, whatever you hear from Don Hagen about me, ignore it. In fact, don't talk to Hagen about us. Trust me. I don't want anything to mess us up before we really get the chance to know each other. And there's one other thing. This is my room-mate's place. The arrangement we have is I don't introduce her to strange faces at breakfast. So you're not staying the night, until you've met her. And she comes in from Boise, Idaho, round dawn.'

'That's a long, very nice speech, but it's not what I came for.'

She laughed. 'Then hurl your pants off, pal, and let's get to it . . .'

He crawled out of bed, had coffee. Made another cup, blacker. Still felt disoriented. It was just past eight o'clock. The phone rang.

'John, you up?' Hagen's voice sounded as if it was being strained through gravel.

'I'm up.'

'Where you been, kid?' Hagen sounded bored and ill.

'Boston. M.I.T.'

'Oh, really?' He didn't sound too interested. 'What happened – you left the safe house?'

'Safe from what?'

'Good question,' Hagen conceded.

'Here's another one. When are you going to straight with me?'

'Some gratitude. I've been putting in hours for you.'

'Doing what?'

'Why don't we meet? I want to do something with you.'

'Where?'

'Can you get over to Phillips Drive? It's off Coldwater. Don't arrive like the Eighth Army. I'm on surveillance.'

'When?'

'Now.'

'It'll take me an hour.'

'I'll be here.'

It took Dolan an hour and a quarter to battle with the traffic up Santa Monica, with a lot of checking with his watch. Hagen was often very precise with his appointments – if the invited person didn't show up at the precise time, Hagen would often take off.

He found Phillips Drive near the top of Coldwater. There was a blue Pontiac sedan parked just into the street. Hagen alone in it. Dolan turned the Chrysler off Coldwater, tucked it in behind the Pontiac, got out and joined the cop.

'You look like a piece of shit,' Hagen offered.

'Lower the windows. It smells like a Turkish brothel. Did you sleep in this automobile?'

'I don't sleep any more, John. I just worry about you.' Hagen said it flatly. 'Look at that.' He pointed.

Dolan looked across Coldwater Canyon in the direction the cop had indicated. There was a chauffeur in a parked Rolls Royce in the curb down from some expensive houses. 'So?'

'The chauffeur's name is Benno Mollo.'

'So?'

'What strikes you about him?'

'Not a lot.'

Hagen shrugged. 'So, right. He's a chauffeur in a peaked hat, chauffeur's uniform, sitting in a parked Rolls Royce outside a bunch of expensive homes. You know what he's doing?'

'He's reading the *L.A. Times*, and I don't care what he's doing.'

'He's not reading the *L.A. Times*. He's not a chauffeur. And he owns the Rolls Royce. He's a burglar. And he's making notes about movements in and out of those expensive houses. And when he's checked them out for a few days, then he'll take the homes apart.'

Dolan studied the burglar, fifty yards away, back to him, sitting in the Rolls. 'So what do you do?'

'Watch him. He turned up here first time yesterday. He'll watch today and tomorrow. Maybe hit on Saturday. Saturday's a good day for burglarizing. A lot of these head for out of town.'

'Listen, this is fascinating to you, but I got problems of my own.'

'Sure,' Hagen said lightly. 'But stand back from them, John. Then maybe you'll identify the jokers in the pack. Like the chauffeur who's really a burglar. You know we had another big burglar in two months back. We can hang all his work together by his *modus operandi*. We think he's earned himself a couple a million in a two-year operation.'

'Another time, Don. I got other things on my mind.'

'I got your problems in front of me. We're going to City Hall.'

'City Hall?'

'I'll tell you.'

'What about your burglar?'

'Saturday we'll have his gonads on a plate, fried, madeira sauce. If we're lucky. I feel lucky.'

'I don't.'

'You've a problem we're going to solve, give or take a dead dog or two.'

Hagen put the car into gear and nosed it left out into the canyon and downhill away from the Rolls Royce burglar.

'Let me tell you about our friendship,' Hagen offered. Then he paused, concentrated on finding a way past an ageing blonde in a ship-length Cadillac convertible. 'No. Let's hear it the other way round. John Dolan, you tell me about our friendship.'

Dolan considered it. There was a way, a route towards some fundamental questions he wanted to ask. It wasn't that Hagen was sensitive to any approach. But he'd a talent to parry, in offhandedness, the direct question. Dolan felt it was time to get certain items completely straight. 'You know, I've told you a dozen times, I never hit any of the four guys in our bar fight with a terrific left. You've always insisted I did. It's like the basis of your goodness to me is founded on a mistake. But you won't have it. You know? Why?'

'Pass,' Hagen said genially.

'And now you say, "Pass".'

'Why not?'

'Let's talk about that.'

'Go.'

'The only time we meet is when you phone and say, meet me here, meet me there. You're almost always alone.'

'So?'

'I don't know anything about the rest of your life. This is what I suspect. I suspect you got a thousand close and intimate friends. Like hundreds of cop colleagues, like the other people you get drunk with, like Christa Beecham.'

'A thousand?' Hagen was looking at him quizzically. 'What's the point you're making?'

'If I'm one in a thousand, Don, I might not be that important.'

'How come?'

'I . . . think I'm not that important.'

'Why?'

'Because you hold things back from me.'

'Hold back what?'

'Who told you to put Stone on to me?'

Hagen shrugged, did some more driving, squeezed the car down the side of a couple of trucks wandering loose near the junction with Sunset Boulevard. 'You're not one in a thousand, John.'

'Answer my question.'

'Yep.' Hagen didn't for a moment. 'We're going to

City Hall,' he said as he swung the car left on to Sunset.

'You told me.'

'Here's the answer.' Hagen accelerated the car to ten miles above the legal limit. 'I need the total cooperation of P.D. to get me off this shoot-out rap. They'll hang me. I'll get best counsel. They'll be brave. But at this moment in time I got to be Lord Fauntleroy. You know what that means?'

'What?'

'I was told to shut up by the guy who ordered me to phone you to call Joseph Stone.'

'So you're not going to tell me who ordered you to phone me?'

'I'm not going to tell you, but I love you,' Hagen said easily. 'Next. I think it's evens if I get busted out of the Force after the trial. So I do what I'm told, but basically I don't give a shit any more for the Department. You understand, prick, to P.D. I'm obedient, but I swear to you, quietly I'm investigating your droll business, and eventually I'll get a result. Moderato Cantabile, John, I'm going to get a result for you.'

'So that's brush-off number one,' Dolan said coldly. 'Now tell me about Christa.'

'Christa Beecham?'

'Christa who-else?'

Hagen smiled. 'Good-looking kid. She started out to be an actress. Recently divorced. I don't know a hell of a lot more about her.'

'Stop the car.'

'Why?'

'Stop the car.'

Hagen braked the car and pulled it into the curb. 'Now what?'

'Why are we going to City Hall?'

'We're going to the Civic Legal Department.

There's a Japanese type lady there. I'm trying to pull her but she gives me such a bad time, that when I succeed I'm going to say to her – I'm going to step back from her, and say, "Lady, there's one thing I can't take about this Police Department work, and it's sexual harassment!" You know, she's one of those frigid teasers.'

'Shut up, Don . . .' Dolan was near despairing. 'Why are we going to the Civic Legal Department?'

'We're going there to lodge a P.D. Deceased Inquiry form.'

'And that's?'

'They handle probate on wills. We get to see all papers to do with the probate on Leon Markovicz' estate.'

'What does that do for us?'

Hagen looked pained. 'I'll tell you. We had a little old lady, murdered, near you, near Venice. She looked like a poor little old lady, until a bill for half a million bucks' worth of insurance, for jewellery, was sent in to probate. So suddenly we had the motive for the murder. She'd been murdered and her jewellery stolen. The craziest things turn up for probate at Civic Legal Department. Let's see what's turned up for this Markovicz.'

'Don, I'm not feeling too happy about anything that's going on, and your motives.'

'Shame on you.'

'I'll get a cab back to my car. You go to the Japanese lady. There's one other thing I want you to do for me.'

'You got me all wrong.'

'The new head of Markovicz' old department at M.I.T. is a guy named Sydney Gower. I want you to run a check on him for me.'

'Wait a minute.' Hagen gave a sour laugh. 'You want to run a check. D'you think you work for the shitting Police Department?'

'The shitting Police Department is your bag. Dean Sydney Gower – who is he? What background?' Dolan got out of the car, slammed the passenger door, and strode off up the street. A minute later he found a cab and was heading back for Venice and wondering why he hadn't told Hagen about the videocassette from Mrs Markovicz, or that Stone had an appointment at noon to buy the notebooks. He didn't wonder about it long. It was tit for tat. He was convinced Hagen was holding out on him. He would hold out on Hagen.

Back at the house he phoned the local xerox store. He told them he had eleven notebooks, forty pages each, to copy. They told him they'd be free to do it if he came by in half an hour.

He had half an hour hanging heavy on his hands. There was a new wine list from an Italian liquor mart in Anaheim. He dialled the number.

'Yes?'

'Euro Liquor Inc?'

'That's us.'

'Is Mr Benito Lucca there?'

'Who want's him?'

'*Village West*, John Dolan.'

'Hold.'

Half a minute later the proprietor came on. 'Yes?' The voice was sharp.

'John Dolan. I'm wine correspondent for *Village West*. Perhaps you've seen my column?'

'What's your enquiry, Mr Dolan?'

'I got your wine list this morning. By coincidence, I'm just doing a piece on chianti. You know, there's a lot of "for and against" at the moment, particularly the D.O.C. requirement that Malvasia and Trebbiano grapes be included.'

'That's a lot of crap.' The liquor store owner sounded like a member of the Teamsters' Union.

'Could be. The point is, I see you have some Ricasoli Brolio '80. As it happens, I haven't had the opportunity to taste the '80's . . .'

'So you'd like me to send you a couple of cases?'

'Well, that would be extremely civil.'

'You know you wine writers baff me off!' The man's voice exploded in fury. 'Your fucking impudence. You think a plug in some shitty column in *Village West* would sell even one bottle of my wine? Go fuck yourself! D'you know it's an offence in the State of California to beg on the phone?'

Dolan heard the receiver crack down at the other end. He shrugged. Some you lose.

He went out to the car, drove the half mile to the xerox store. He sat on the corner while a young black guy copied the eleven notebooks on to four hundred and forty sheets of paper.

He went back to face Stone.

Stone arrived dead on twelve. He walked in the front door carrying a briefcase, followed Dolan into the still half reassembled wreckage of the living room. 'What the shit happened here?'

Dolan's two attempts to clear the mess had not panned out. 'I was burglarized.'

'Burglarized!' Stone sounded horrified. 'The notebooks . . .!'

'Here.' Dolan patted the pile of books.

A cautious but pleased smile came over Stone's face. 'What did the burglars take?'

'Nothing much.'

'And you've talked to nobody about our transactions?'

'You said not to.'

'I said not to.'

'It's not a transaction till I see your money.'

Stone opened the briefcase solemnly on top of the notebooks. 'Count it.'

Dolan glanced at the bundles of used twenty-bills inside. 'I'll take your word for it.'

'Don't take my word for it.'

'I'll take your word for it. Now why don't you check what you're paying fifty grand for?'

'An associate will do that. I want to confirm the second part of the deal. You will make yourself available some time in the next week to go out of town somewhere, with my associate, for three, four days, to go through these notes with him at a *per diem* of three thousand a day.'

'Sounds okay.'

'Good.'

'I've no plans. You want coffee?'

'I'll go,' Stone said busily, as if he was a traveller in toilet articles and he had twenty stores to visit. 'You'll get a message, where and when.' Stone was putting the notebooks back into the briefcase.

'My time is your time.'

'Good to do business with you.'

'Mutual.'

Stone turned to head for the door, paused. 'Hey, you wouldn't have done anything crazy, like make a copy of these notebooks?'

'You think I'd do that? Listen, if you want the mallulah back, I'm an eccentric millionaire. Also I was thinking maybe if they're worth fifty to you, maybe I should shop around. You want your money back, Mr Stone?'

'No,' Stone said sharply. 'I'll be in touch.' And he was gone out of the door into a black Lincoln convertible, which took off with leisurely acceleration.

Dolan went back in, sat down, and looked at the money. He didn't consider it belonged to him. This was some kind of game, like Monopoly. He didn't know the rules, could just about identify the other players, but not their motives. The likelihood was that he would lose the game, so the fifty grand might as well be toy money. He got an old 'David's Cookies' tin out of a kitchen cupboard, put the cash inside, and stored the tin under the sink. He went upstairs and took the sheets off the bed, and collected the towels from the two bathrooms.

The phone rang. It was Julie. There was anger and a little hint of hysteria in her voice. He reckoned she'd just got up after some booze or dope sleep. 'I had a burglary last night.'

'I had a burglary yesterday,' Dolan reprised.

'No kidding?'

'No kidding. What did they take?'

'That's the point.'

'What point?'

'Shut up and listen to me.' Her voice was cold and hard. 'Nothing.'

'Nothing?'

'For Jesus sake, stop repeating what I say. They took nothing, but they fucked my place. Looks like a grenade in every room.'

A slow, cold, minuscule shiver had begun a spinal ascent up towards his brain. Two burglaries, two hours' flying time apart, and copycat. Obviously the burglaries had been ordered up from the same source. A source that could command the services of several burglars.

'I nearly caught 'em – walked straight in on the mothers . . .'

'You did what?'

'Walked straight in. Four fucking burglars, all in the den. Ripping the place apart. They kind of sprinted out – just sort of jogged past me, got into a Chevy brake, and drove off.'

'The Markovicz notes?'

'No, I got them at the wine bar.'

'You didn't get the licence? The Chevy?'

'What are you, a cop or something?'

'Yes or no?'

'No.'

'Cops? Did you call them?'

Pause, Then, 'I don't like cops, Johnno, as you know.'

'You didn't call the cops?'

'Sometimes, honey, I feel you need a deaf aid. I don't fuck with cops.'

'What about your red-haired boyfriend, the butcher? Matisse?'

'The cunt slept through it.'

'Your language is appalling.'

'Shut your fucking mouth.'

'Give me a description of the four guys and I can pass it on to a cop I know.'

'Bollocks.'

They both went quiet a moment. 'Listen, Stone came by. What d'you think? He gave me fifty in twenty-notes. Fifty grand.'

'Fifty!' She laughed.

'What's funny?'

'Fifty. And you accepted it? Did you give him the notebooks?'

'Yes. What's funny?'

'I cooled him. Then I asked him . . . I asked him,' she laughed unpleasantly. 'He agreed. A hundred. He flies up tonight to give me a hundred grand!'

That worried Dolan.

'You're a dumb son-of-a-bitch.'

'Maybe your notes are more legible than mine. You know, neater . . .'

She laughed again, hollowly. 'There's something else. You remember that prick Colville, Dennis Colville?'

'Yes.'

'In the double-breasted suits and the right-wing politics.'

Dolan had forgotten the double-breasted suits. 'What?'

'He phoned. He's been contacted by Stone. Offered fifty for his Markovicz notes.'

'Okay.'

'Okay what?'

'Nothing.'

'He's a worm. I don't trust him. he was the only one of us who maybe knew what Leon was talking about.'

'And Mrs Markovicz.'

'Did she?'

'Where's Colville live?'

'I got a phone number L.A.'

'I'll get a pad.' He found a ballpoint. She gave him the number. 'Did Colville want to speak to me?'

'He didn't say. Didn't ask for your phone.'

'Hey . . .'

'Yes?'

'Have your butcher present and correct when Stone comes. Stone is an ex-mobster, not even ex.'

'So?'

'Don't think you can best him, Julie, you're not that bright.' He meant it as advice and not as an insult.

'You're crazy from hunger. Get your head back in your ass where it belongs.' She rang off.

He looked at Colville's number, debated. He picked up the phone and dialled. He was unsure whether he was pleased when the thin, reedy voice of Colville came on.

'Two-seven-oh-eight.'

'It's John Dolan.'

A pause as if Colville was also working out whether he was pleased to hear Dolan's voice. 'I was talking to your wife, John. Julie . . .' He offered the name as if Dolan might have forgotten it.

'She tells me.'

'This Markovicz business.'

'Exactly.'

'Why were you at M.I.T. yesterday asking for me?'

'You got my message?'

'I got it.'

'Davis was fun. The old times were the good times, yes? I even miss the Jimmy Carter Presidency.'

'Not even Jimmy Carter does that, Dolan.'

'That's funny,' Dolan said dryly. 'Glad you kept your sense of humour, Dennis. Listen, d'you think I should tell you I just parted with my Markovicz notes for fifty grand, and Julie says not to tell you that she's gone in to bat for a hundred for hers, and Stone loves it, and is going north today to pay her?'

'A hundred?' Colville sounded surprised and irritated. 'You sure, a hundred? You positive?'

'Keep in touch . . .'

'Listen, I want to talk to you.' Suddenly the reedy voice was sharp. 'You live in Venice, right?'

'We get a better class of burglar here, steals nothing.'

'I can get to you in twenty minutes. Please, can I come and talk to you?'

'Look, I had a small problem with a dead dog, and I have to put my sheets through the laundromat. Unless you've got some spare sheets, king size. I've always been meaning to buy some good sheets, My other pair were shredded by a laundry that cleans with a Caterpillar earth mover.'

'What are you talking about?'

'There's a Bendix laundromat corner of Alto and First. Meet me there.'

'Okay.'

Dolan took the xerox copy of his notes, put it in an empty wine box, placed a half dozen bottles of gut rot Almedan on top, stowed it down the basement with some of his older wine. The burglars had not wrecked the wine cellar, and had left all the cases unopened.

He walked with his plastic bag containing the brown-blooded sheets to the laundromat. It was empty. When Colville arrived a quarter of an hour later, they still had the place to themselves.

'Hello, John . . .'

Dolan could gauge the man was making some special effort to be pleasant. He couldn't remember Colville as a person who smiled easily. Colville was trying out a smile now. Dolan shook the offered hand.

'How long since we last met?' Colville enquired.

'Year and a half, maybe?'

'Poor Leon Markovicz . . .'

'You haven't heard from Mrs Markovicz recently? I've been trying to phone her.'

'Nope. Don't you have a washing machine?'

'Divorced.'

Colville put up another weak smile, nodded towards the corner. 'That machine make anything drinkable?'

'Coffee-flavoured detergent.'

'Want one?'

'Why not?'

Colville went and put coins in the machine, returned with two plastic cups of coffee. 'So how about this fifty grand, hundred grand offer for our lecture notes?'

'You tell me. Julie and I sat through those lectures because we pitied him, and I was pulling her. And she felt, once we got to meet Leon socially, and Greta Markovicz – there was no sloughing off. Julie had less botany or biology than me. I was ace at both subjects at school.'

'So you stuck out the lectures and you didn't know what he was speaking about?'

'Did you?'

'Pretty much.'

'That's terrific news. Tell me what Leon was lecturing about?'

'You serious?'

'I'm serious.'

'I think you're kidding me.'

'I'm not.'

'His special interest was plant genetics, cloning, all that stuff, in relation to root stock. There's a lot of work going on in genetic engineering. But it's like heart transplants – everything's been worked out in theory, but the mechanics is something else.'

'Is that it?'

'That's it.'

'What are the commercial applications of Leon's work?'

Colville gave a wry little laugh. 'Commercial applications? Nothing at the moment. I imagine at some point the work might be at the basis of something. Rutherford in Cambridge had no idea splitting an atom might end up as a nice fat bomb. Take my word for it. As of this moment I don't know of any commercial application, except to keep a lot of guys in work in a lot of laboratories in a lot of nations.'

It was too easy an answer. Dolan had the sense that even Colville didn't think he was getting away with it. But more to the point, he was positive Colville wasn't about to level with him. 'Now you. Stone's offered you fifty?'

'Yes.'

'And?'

'I'm . . . thinking about it.'

'I mean, your notes would make a lot more sense.'

'I can't believe you sat in a classroom for twelve months and didn't understand what the shit he was talking about.'

'No,' Dolan corrected, 'don't remember now what he was talking about. But I did copy from the blackboard. Did Stone say to you that after the purchase of the notes . . .'

'I have to talk to some guy to go through them.'

'At a *per diem*?'

'What were you offered?'

'Three thousand bucks a day.'

'This is all crazy. Ever since Stone called, I've been thinking about it. But believe me, John, I knew Leon's territory. There's no commercial application for his work.'

Dolan nodded easily. 'Right.' Colville was enemy. Colville was lying.

'You got to do me a favour, John.'

'Go ahead.'

'I'm beginning to move in a fairly cultured circle.'

'That's good news.'

'Don't send me up, pal,' Colville said gently. 'Point is, the kind of social people I'm moving with now. All the gossip is about antiques and Californian wine. Is it good? Is it great? Is it as good as the wines of France? You know?'

'I know.'

'You're the wine writer. You're the expert. Get me a couple of cases of California wine, and a couple of the best books on it. I mean, go as expensive as you want. I want the best. Then I'll sit down, read the books, drink the wine. Then I'll be able to do all this social chat with the smart set I'm moving with.'

You poor bastard, Dolan thought. He said, 'I'll do that.'

'Are you going to forget?'

'There's a place not far from here. I'll do it after my wash day.'

'Drop me a note at M.I.T. about what you selected, why, and the bill for what I owe you.'

'I always thought you were a pretty boring little guy, Dennis. I'm delighted I was wrong, that you aspire to the higher things. I'll get you two cases of the finest wine in California – and definitive texts. You'll amaze your friends.' He smiled into the glowering face of the scientist.

He made a point of getting Colville's wine. After the laundromat he drove to Encino. Reuben Weiss of Reuben's Wine Store owed him some money. He wouldn't get it till Reuben was ready to pay, but a reminder would be in order, and he had other things to discuss with his major employer.

Reuben as usual was skulking out the back of the store in the huge air-conditioned Nissen huts he'd largely built with his own hands.

'How's business?'

'Good for me is good for you. How are you doing?'

'It's all work,' Dolan said gently.

'Everything's work, pal. It's the definition of work. For me, it's twenty-fours hours a day. For you, it's twenty-four hours a month.'

Reuben was sixtyish, small and fat. He'd come from Seattle, and should have stayed there, because six months a year he couldn't take the temperature in Los Angeles, and had to towel his face and neck dry to the tune of two boxes of kleenex a day. He had a kleenex out now in the air-conditioned Nissen, as he took his stock book up and down the rows of wine crates.

'You got the '82's, clarets, yet?'

'Two months. They're still looking great.'

'Getting shippers' bottles?'

'Some.'

'I'd like to taste.'

'Don't think you can work the same seam with me, that I'm working with you.'

'Okay.' Dolan shrugged. 'Anything you want, I can get.'

Reuben paused to think. Dolan studied him. In Dolan's eyes Reuben knew more about wine than anyone he'd ever met. He'd started out as a merchant seaman. he'd gone to Cunard, and had ended up on the great liners – the Queen Mary, the Queen Elizabeth. In those days Cunard had the largest wine cellars in the world. Reuben had scrubbed decks by day, and done a deal with the ship's sommelier whereby he got the remains of the bottles of the great wines served to the first-class passengers, late at night. He read voraciously about wine. The ships cruised to every country in the world. In each country Reuben tasted the wines. Age fifty, he went into the wine business, as a shipper. Now he was shipping, and retailing. But he still liked a bargain, and Dolan provided him with reasonable bargains.

'You sent me two grand, but you still owe me money.'

'My credit's good,' Reuben countered.

'It's my credit's that's not great, that's why I mention you owe me.'

'Everything in good time, pal. Now what can you get me that I can sell?'

'Tell me.'

'I'm able to move fast, Vintage '76 champagne. All the wine snots in Beverly Hills are comparative listing it against the '75.'

'Right.'

'Now I'm so busy, I can be rude. Go away.'

'No. I'm going to buy some of your Californian best, two cases.' He explained to Reuben about Colville. Reuben advised on the order. Dolan ended up with a half case of Château Montelena '77, and six bottles of Ridge Vineyards *petit sirah*, and some Mondavi Cabernet Reserve, and Mayacamas Chardonnay.

He drove home, left the wine in the car, took the washing indoors. He ran the message machine. It offered a number for where Hagen would be until one o'clock. Dolan dialled. 'Don Hagen there?'

'Don Hagen is talking to you.' Hagen sounded thoughtful, quiet. 'Your pal, Dean Sydney Gower, Department of Biological Sciences. He's a lawyer. Quite a well known one.'

'Lawyer? How come a lawyer? How come not a scientist?'

'Wait with the shit.'

'It's not shit.'

'I'll tell you more about him. He was a very important union lawyer. To you, that means nothing. To me, a union lawyer gets characterized as often not far short of a hood. Show me a big union lawyer, I'll show you a guy who has dubious connections. They're all criminals. So now ask your question.'

'What question?'

'The question is, Dolan, why the fuck three months back did they make a union lawyer Dean of the Department of Biological Sciences? And the answer is, Dolan, I'm working on it. Speak to you tomorrow.'

'Wait . . .'

But Hagen had put the phone down.

'Shit,' Dolan said aloud. He redialled Hagen's number. No answer, but he had a picture of Hagen listening to the ringing phone, not answering it because he'd know it was Dolan, and he had nothing more to say.

Dolan went out to the car. In the wine store he'd spotted a bottle of Duckhorn Vineyards Merlot – one he'd never tasted. He took the bottle back into the kitchen and opened it.

He checked the fine wine list that had arrived in the morning mail, dialled a number.

'Eastern Liquor Inc.' A woman's voice answered.

'Mr Maharis, please. John Dolan.'

'Thank you sir, I am connecting you.'

Maharis was an Anatolian with a voice and manner exhausted by living thirty years in America. 'Yes, Mr Dolan?' Brief and to the point, and bored.

'We've met, Mr Maharis – I write the wine seg for *Village West*.'

'Yes, Mr Dolan?'

'I'm doing a piece on vintage champagne. I was wondering how your stocks were loaded. You probably have a lot more '76 than '75?'

'We have plenty '76 . . .'

'As you know, doubts are being cast on the '76 vintage. A lot of folk saying the '75 has the clear lead . . .'

'We don't agree.'

'My view exactly. Well, I'll be writing my piece saying '76 has better everything, fruit, balance, subtlety, finesse . . .'

'I'm a busy guy,' the Turk announced.

'Yes?'

'Get to the point, Mr Dolan. I get a plug if you get what?'

'I'd like to taste some '76's.'

'By taste, do I take it you mean a case?'

'Well,' Dolan offered some lightness in pleasure in his voice, 'well, that's more than generous.'

'Give me your address.'

Dolan gave an address and some words of thanks in anticipation. The Turk's voice sounded tireder than it had when he started the exchange.

Dolan put down the phone. There was something wrong with the fifty grand in notes in the 'David's Cookies' tin under the sink. Somehow it wasn't his. A feeling that if he went out to spend it he'd be shot in the head. So carry on the life's work – the routine of the liquor store calls.

He phoned Christa. There was no answer.

He went into the kitchen, poured hot water from the tap over instant rice, threw it into a pan with a couple of eggs, some honey, and freeze-dried onion rings, and burned the mess up into an omelette. He'd eaten half of it when the phone rang.

'Listen.' Hagen's voice sounded troubled. 'We should get together.'

'What is it?'

'Mrs Markovicz is dead. Killed by a truck in Napa an hour ago. One-seventeen p.m.'

Dolan took in the information, shaken, but quiet, looking for some logic in marshalling the impact of the news, its relevance to himself, its relevance to his feelings about the mad lady. He was confused. 'What happened?' he said at last.

Hagen's voice, lower, more sober than Dolan ever remembered it, started listing the events. She had been in the El Paso Hotel restaurant in Napa. She'd had a long breakfast. And quite a few drinks, alone. She'd been presented with the bill. She'd told the waiter she'd sit on in the restaurant until lunch, when somebody would be picking her up. The maitre d' had talked to her, said they wanted to close and clean the restaurant – that at eleven-thirty – could she leave? She'd gotten aggressive, shouted about all waiters being Nazis, and the maitre d' had gone off and left her there. At midday she'd moved to the adjoining bar. Two cleaners and the barman saw two men – they had given descriptions. Neither fitted Stone. They were well dressed. They came and sat with her. Some quiet, almost whispered conversation turned into a one-sided argument, and she started screaming at them. The two cleaners and barman couldn't say what they had been talking about, just that her abuse was general bad language. After ten minutes of altercation the three left. The windows overlooked the street. The cleaners could see the three continue the row out in the curb. A limousine pulled in, another guy got out. The three had then tried to bundle Mrs Markovicz into the automobile. But she'd backed off, had turned and run drunkenly off across the street. A truck had hit her. She was dead when the ambulance arrived. The three men were gone in the limousine as soon as the truck hit her. 'When did you last see her?' Hagen wanted to know.

'When she came with the dog.' Dolan was debating the number of personnel now involved in events. Four burglars at Julie's. Maybe two, three, four at his place. Three guys at the Mrs Markovicz scene, two arguing with her, one in a limousine. 'What d'you think?' he said sharply.

'I mean, it might not be anything more sinister than Mrs M. arguing with some guys, running into the road, and greeting a truck. But in package with two burglaries, a stabbed dog, this guy Stone, and other events, I worry.'

'When you stop worrying, are you going to be able to help me sort this shit out?'

'What d'you think I'm doing? I'm following Stone at the moment.'

Dolan could hear his own voice go tense. 'Why are you following Stone?'

'Stick with me, kid. I'll get your answers.'

'No, I don't believe you any more, Don. I don't trust you.' But he was speaking to a dead line. Hagen had put down the phone.

He phoned 'Information', got the number for Hunt's Winery, and dialled it. He spent the next two hours hanging around waiting for Hunt's personal private secretary to ring back with a time for an appointment.

He woke early and had to lie there a moment working out an agenda for picking himself up, picking Christa up, and getting to the airport.

He phoned Christa. 'Are you ready to go?'

'Yes.' She sounded pleased.

'Be with you in half an hour.'

'Listen, John. I'll get a cab to the airport. Save you a trip.'

'It's not a problem.'

'I insist.'

He didn't tell her about Mrs Markovicz' death. At Arrowhead, and subsequently, he didn't think he'd talked about Mrs Markovicz.

She was in good spirits on the flight to San Francisco. She said she was wearing her divorce court outfit, a careful assembly of sober dark tweed. She looked stunning. 'Is he an interesting millionaire?'

'I don't know. I said a dozen words to him.'

'I might marry him. It's time I married wealth. Wine writers are out of vogue.'

A half hour into the flight, she said, 'You're depressed, right? It makes you boring.'

'I feel I'm being eaten.'

'Come on, John Dolan. There's been a series of little events. You're unharmed. You've got fifty thousand dollars. There's an explanation for everything. Professor Markovicz has invented a revolutionary new carwash . . .'

'I don't think so . . .'

They landed at San Francisco at noon. Half an hour later they were in a hire car on the road.

The ride to the Hunt estate took two hours. The day was brisk, some of the cold threat of the last week was being warmed out by gentler breezes. As they entered the Napa Valley the low falls of hills were clear of mists.

Approaching from the south and not from the east as on his previous visit, Dolan saw first the long side of the Hunt villa silhouetted on a hill. It was almost completely screened by tall cypresses.

There was a chauffeur just inside the gates. He was carefully dusting the prow of a dark green Bentley. He went ahead of them to the front door. Then they were processed via a butler and a secretary into a high-ceilinged room.

The tall stooping figure of Hunt came forward across a mirror-polish wood floor. 'Nice to meet you again, Mr Dolan.'

'This is Christa Beecham.'

Hunt was already smiling and extending his hand towards her.

So you like a pretty girl, Dolan thought inwardly as he watched Hunt's eyes run up and down Christa's figure.

'What can I offer you?' The tall man crossed the room and opened the doors of an antique parquetry cabinet, to display drinks. 'At this time of day, a glass of sherry?' It was a question to Christa.

She nodded.

'And you, Mr Dolan?'

'I'll have the same.'

Hunt poured the drinks and came back with the two glasses linked between the fingers. 'I was intrigued by your phone call. You came here with Professor Markovicz?'

'Yes.'

'But you're also the wine writer?'

'Yes.'

'When you came with the professor, did you introduce yourself as a correspondent?'

'Yes.'

'I'd forgotten that.' Hunt inclined his head slightly

to one side. 'However, my secretary said this visit, you want to talk to me about the professor?'

'That's right.'

'But what would *I* know about him?'

Dolan changed tack. He didn't want this to become an interrogation. He wanted to ease himself and Christa first through the millionaire's defences. 'Well, maybe there was something that day we came. I'm interested in anything you remember of what he said to you. He was a strange man.'

'Yes.'

'There was a fine mind there.'

'I understand he had a reputation for genius.' Hunt was pursing his lips. 'However, as I say, on the phone, you asked my secretary if you could put some questions to me about the professor. So what are the questions?'

Dolan saw that the man wasn't about to be finessed. 'All right. You invited Leon Markovicz here. He did a juggling act, and I think he showed you inside his grey truck?'

'No,' Hunt said gently. 'He didn't show me inside any truck.'

'I thought he did.'

'No, he didn't.'

Dolan wondered how to ask the man why he was lying. He shrugged. 'I'm sorry, I thought you saw inside the truck.'

'No, I didn't.'

'Can you tell me why you invited him here?'

'Ah.' Hunt's face brightened. 'It was the other way round. It would be accurate to say the professor invited himself.'

'How was that?'

Hunt put on an expression of mild puzzlement. 'I'm not quite sure myself. Let me explain. This estate is a small part of my organization, Hunt

Industries. We have many interests in the fields of electronics. I'm also a benefactor of Davis College, the Oenological Studies Department. They've collaborated with me on hybridization and investigations into root stock. Apparently, Professor Markovicz, when he received his post at Davis, heard of my connection. He asked to see me and demonstrate some invention of his.'

'Invention?'

'I'm going to tell you, Mr Dolan, that I don't know what he had in mind. He prefaced his arrival that day with you, by sending me two letters. Candidly I, and the experts I employ, were unable to make head nor tail of them. But he was a persistent man, and because of my good relations with Davis, I invited him to come. He insisted no other scientists be present. We had lunch. He did some juggling. Then he and I had a talk. And talked about . . . really nothing in particular.'

'So, just idle chat?'

'Idle chat, Mr Dolan – that describes it exactly.'

'I, and others, believe he was on to some quite significant discovery.'

Hunt's eyes studied him unwavering. 'He communicated nothing to me, Mr Dolan. Except the sense that he was a very strange man.' He turned to Christa. 'Did you know him, Miss Beecham?'

'No, I never met him.'

'The world of the brilliant teacher and scholar is a paradoxical one. It seems to me, the more brilliant, the less the ability to communicate. Let me refill your glasses.'

Dolan surrendered his glass and moved over to the wall to examine a parchment map framed in glass above the fireplace. It was a crude map of some unidentifiable Greek islands.

'That's a Mercator,' Hunt said, not looking up from pouring the drinks.

Dolan studied the projection lines. 'Yes, I see that.'

'No, I mean a Mercator original.' He handed Christa her glass, and then came over and stood by Dolan. 'Many forget that Mercator started as a young man by mapping the coasts of Italy. Then he went on to the Dalmatian coast. Then Greece.' His voice had the easy sureness of a lecturer. 'It's said his projection came from his growing dementia about getting those coastlines to fit together.' He shrugged. 'Another unorthodox and brilliant man.'

Dolan studied the fading ink lines on the map. 'There was a whole century of mariners charting coastlines, wasn't there? People with the craziest ideas, trying to rationalize dreams.'

'We all test the limits of adventure, heroism, endurance, all the time, do we not? We all map coastlines, searching for horizons. And there's another aspect to this business.' Hunt was studying Dolan. 'We also go out and travel far, just in order to make the journey back. On the journey back is the vision, the vision of all we've learned. On the journey back we chart ourselves, the contours of our own souls.'

'Markovicz was on the journey home. He'd made his discovery. He was coming home.'

'What a pity he didn't draw maps which could be understood.'

'I think he did,' Dolan said. 'But they've gone missing.'

The butler came in and announced lunch.

They moved down a corridor and into a whitewashed refectory. Here a long table had been laid with three places. Hunt escorted Christa to her chair and gestured Dolan to sit opposite her. He sat down at the top of the table.

Dolan looked around the room, struck again by the way money had been used throughout the villa to make the effect of simple comfort.

Double doors at the end of the room opened, and a maid appeared pushing a trolley. She transferred silver salvers on to the table and without a word went out. Hunt took the lids off and began to circulate the various dishes. When the others were served, he served himself, with a minute portion which he cut into small pieces. This done he looked up at Dolan. 'So the wine writer has turned into a mystery investigator?'

'It's getting less of a mystery.'

'I'm beyond the age of mystery. All I want is a simple life, and a few friends, and my table to be graced from time to time by a beautiful woman, like Christa here.'

'To return to Leon Markovicz.'

'By all means.'

'D'you have the letters he sent you before his arrival for the juggling session?'

'I don't know. It's possible. I can ask my secretary,' Hunt offered.

'I'd like to see them.'

'I'll see what I can do.'

'Is your secretary here? Can we check this?'

'No, she's away today.'

Dolan looked for a fresh tack around the stonewalling, decided to let it rest for the moment.

'This Macedonia di Frutta,' Hunt had turned to Christa. 'All the fruit is grown on the estate. Pineapples, kiwi, bananas. Organically. It's important.'

'Why's that?' Christa asked.

'Ask the Davis College expert here.' He nodded to Dolan, 'The more exotic the fruit, the more susceptible it is to retention of dieldrin, fungicides, chemicals. The average banana is a package of poison. At my age, one must be careful.'

Dolan studied the man, wondered at his ability to

parry questions with easy banalities, wondered if somehow this might be a key talent for a successful businessman.

Five minutes later, Hunt announced, 'Now for the vintages.'

He led them through long corridors out to the rear of the house, and across a grass and cobbled yard and into the chais, a group of cold buildings next to the north wing. In one chais there was a curved room with flagged stone floor, a long table, and some creaking wooden seats. They sat down and Hunt talked vintages while the butler brought different estate wines for sampling. At the end of an hour they each had about a half dozen glasses in front of them. They felt mildly intoxicated as they left the cellars.

'I hope you enjoyed our wine and company. I'm sorry I wasn't able to help you on the other matter.'

'A wonderful lunch, and I enjoyed it very much,' Christa told the man.

'You will come again,' Hunt decided. He led them through the house out to the hired car. 'I'll ask my secretary if she has the letters from the professor. As I say, I'm sorry I couldn't have helped you more.'

Christa got into the car. Dolan stood by the driver's door. 'You couldn't help me. And that fits the pattern.'

Hunt's eyes narrowed. 'I don't understand, Mr Dolan.'

'And I'm trying to. Markovicz dies. His wife dies. Mysterious people want to buy his students' lecture notes. I go to M.I.T. The head of the School of Biological Sciences has been replaced. Replaced by a union lawyer, Mr Hunt. A hard man. You, an efficient businessman, are not quite sure if your secretary kept two letters. You know what I'm thinking?'

'Tell me, Mr Dolan.'

'I'm beginning to think that what Leon was on to, was so mind-freaking in its implications that it could cause all this: burglaries, deaths, heads of departments being replaced. And your silence.'

'I don't really have anything more to say to you.' Hunt's words were flat, distanced.

'Exactly. So you're some kind of confirmation of some sort. So in that way you've been quite helpful. Thank you.' Dolan got into the car, put the key in the ignition.

'You may be making a mistake pursuing these enquiries, Mr Dolan.' Hunt's voice was cold, hard.

'It's too late, Mr Hunt. I am.' He started the car, drove it across the cobbled entrance, and headed back down the narrow road for the highway.

It was five p.m. when they got back to L.A. Airport.

They walked to Carpark Three at Pan Am and got into the Chrysler. He didn't at once move the car, let the engine warm, and looked at her.

'Yes?'

'I think I have to get in the sack with you.'

She shrugged mildly. She'd been thoughtful on the trip south, had hardly said a word on the plane. 'Okay.'

'Your place or my place?'

'My place.'

'My place. I don't want the watch-watching performance, trying to make it before your flatmate appears.'

She gave a little shrug. 'Okay.'

He drove to Venice. He told her about the tiny house, his tiny mother, the tiny furniture – but the regular-size beds with linen fresh and unironed from the local Bendix laundromat. He told her about Colville – a prick scientist. She laughed, and told him she loved him. She said it in an embarrassed kind of way, ingenuous and like a child talking to a parent. He described the state of the house, the mess of both the dying dog and the wrecker burglars. She turned the whole description into a joke. They were laughing when he led her to the front door, and put the key in the lock.

'Jesus!'

The place had been torn apart. Carpets ripped up, book shelves pulled over, even the cupboards in the kitchen, tins of food hurled across the room, the fridge overturned and leaking milk and broken eggs across other mess on the floor.

The answering machine had been taken from its usual place, the shelf on top of the air-conditioner, and placed in the centre of the floor. It blinked its red light. There was a message on it. Dolan rewound the tape, pressed the transmit button. Stone's voice came on, cold and hard. 'Dolan, you piece of crap. You try to two-time me, boy, you get hit! We took your professor's notes to a lab. We put them under a fluoroscope. It's something for detecting gases. Don't ask me what gas, but a Xerox machine gives off some gas which the fluoroscope picked up. So you xeroxed the notes like I told you not to. So we visited and found one xerox copy under a wine box. We also found your fifty grand in a cookie tin. But that's yours. The prof's notes are now ours. Ours! If you've got a second xerox copy you'd better come across with it. You've been a big disappointment to me. Even so, we go through with the rest of the deal. After the weekend, I phone you. We go and meet this guy to whom you explain as best you can what you've written in these notes. Don't fuck with me, Dolan. You're an amateur.'

Dolan was looking as Christa. Christa was looking thoughtful. 'Phone Don Hagen.'

'From your place. This place depresses me. Burglars come in and out at will.'

She consulted her watch, as if timing had something to do with it. 'You can't stay the night.'

'I'll take what I can get.'

He drove to Laurel Canyon, to the narrow house on the slope screened by the tall trees owned by its more affluent neighbours. She hesitated with the keys at the door. 'Come in. But I am tired. You leave in two hours.'

'Dandy.'

She smiled. 'You know you come up with a lot of Disney words when you get in the sex area.'

They went in. He took off his jacket as the house heat hit him. Without her invitation, sat down in a brown suede armchair.

'Scotch?'

He nodded.

'Phone Don Hagen.'

'I don't know. All I'll get is his answering machine. I'll chase him up later.'

She went over to the bar and pulled out a bottle of Teacher's. 'I feel rough. Too much wine at Hunt's. How do you feel?'

He wondered at the nervous formality of small talk. 'Like that.'

'My room-mate is definitely back at midnight.'

'You told me.' He put the drink down, crossed to her, put his arms around her. He could feel her body tense. Then suddenly her resistance went.

'Like the man said on your phone, you're a shit.' She made an attempt at an encouraging smile. 'I don't think you're an amateur.'

They headed upstairs into the main bedroom.

They didn't make love immediately. Looking back at it later, trying to re-examine her behaviour and motives that night, he concluded that there were various alternatives. That she'd got him talking in the naive assumption that she'd get his mind away from sex, then get him to leave sooner without screwing her. Alternatively, she was deliberately playing with fire, based on some private courageous resolve, now that he was physically in her presence, to try and make a profound change in her life. And maybe her talk about loving him was true. It was about nine o'clock when he told her, almost ordered her, to take her clothes off. And they made love.

At half past nine she said he must go. He was lying naked on top of the bed and he started to protest. She became insistent. And then suddenly below they heard the front door open, and Christa grabbed up her bathrobe and put it on fast, and he pulled the eiderdown from the bottom of the bed up to cover his body. 'Room-mate?'

'Get up,' Christa whispered, her voice desperate.

'What's wrong?'

'Get up!' She said it urgently again. But already it was too late.

'Christa? You upstairs?' It was the sound of a man's voice.

'Well, shit this,' Dolan said sourly. 'So "room-mate"'s male. Why didn't you tell me?' But his protest tailed away because he couldn't understand why Christa was standing there, her body shaking.

Colville entered the room, stopped short, shocked. It took full seconds before his expression moved from blankness to suffused fury. 'What the fuck are you doing here?' Then to Christa, 'Jesus, did I say you could go this far?!'

It was a different Colville from the one Dolan had teased early morning in the laundromat.

Dolan got up, pulled on his trousers, zipped them. He was as angry as Colville, and as furious at her.

He left them, went down the stairs to the living room, picked up his coat and jacket, put them on hurriedly, walked out of the house, and slammed the door.

He drove back to L.A. Airport. Inside he picked up a ticket for the last flight back to San Francisco. He found a booth and dialled Julie. His breath missed a beat when she answered the phone.

'Yes?'

'John. I'm coming up. I've got to see you.'

'You in L.A.?'

'About to get on a plane.'

She detected the anger in his voice, puzzled that it didn't seem to be directed at her. 'What is it?'

'The whole thing is some fucking conspiracy. It involves cops, M.I.T., Hunt, Colville. Plus I was set up with the broad who lives with Colville. Why?'

'Have you any idea what the fuck you're talking about?'

'Are you part of this shit?'

'What shit?'

'Either you're part of it, and you're going to tell me what it is, or you're not, and the two of us have to get together to find out what scam is going on here.'

'Hey, did you get paid?'

He realized now her voice was slurred. Doped, or drunk.

'Fifty grand cash. Stone, today.'

'You gave him the notebooks?'

'Yes.'

'Clown.' A note of triumph in her voice. 'Stone's bringing me a hundred grand later.'

'You're going to be there?'

'I'm waiting for my money.'

He put down the phone, went to a bar, quickly had a scotch, then got on the plane.

It was the same stewardess who'd accompanied him and Christa on the trip from San Francisco. She'd served some wine to the quiet-looking couple. Now she asked Dolan if he wanted more wine, and when he said no, went into some smiling provocation in some questions about where was his lady friend, and an inference that he was going back to San Fran to grab more action. Dolan cooled her off with a single look. She scuttered off to the back of the almost empty plane.

At the terminal the Hertz counter was deserted. He picked up the two phones in the booth, and right-guessed by dialling zero on each of them. The second one answered, and he said sharply he wanted a car, and tonight. A guy, buttoning on his Hertz uniform, turned up five minutes later, and tested his irritation on Dolan, and got some sharp words back.

Dolan got in the car and pointed it northwest out of San Francisco. An hour and a half later he hit the rolling night hills of Napa.

It had been raining. The roads were wet. The sky washed and now dry, resonated with light.

He had driven moderate speed, not panicked, but worried, and wanting to take time, cocooned in the car, to try and work some things out. There was no logic to it. It needed more fact or event. Key pieces which would pull the whole thing together were still missing. The metaphor was not complete. What had Markovicz been juggling with, apart from the green rubber balls? The answer to that would be the answer to everything. He decided he was nowhere near the solution.

At one a.m. the first signs for 'Napa' turned up, framed in light on the highway.

He slowed on the outskirts of town, before the main street, pulled in, and was about to take the left turn up the broken path to Julie's house behind the hoardings, when he braked suddenly.

There was a long wheelbase Jaguar, parked directly outside the run-down clapboard house. He sat in the hired car, paused for a moment to make his decision. If Julie had friends, maybe he didn't want to walk in on them. Friends with an expensive car probably meant dope dealers. Those people could get manic at the knock on the door at one a.m.

He was parked thirty yards back from the house, thinking if he was going to sit out Julie's guests leaving, he should back the car further away, when the front door opened, and the three people in the hall were framed in the hard light of an overhead bare bulb.

There was a guy in a chauffeur's uniform. Dolan identified him immediately as Hunt's chauffeur. He'd seen him hanging around a Bentley outside the villa. Then there was Julie, shoulders hunched, looking businesslike, talking fast. Behind, the boyfriend, Matisse, looking crazy, his streaked red hair now collapsed around his head. Matisse was talking too, animatedly, but the chauffeur and Julie were ignoring him. Dolan could hear nothing of what was going on. The chauffeur went to the trunk of the limousine, unlocked it, took out a briefcase, brought it back, handed it to Julie, who opened it. The red-haired boyfriend now stumbled forwards. There was a sharp exchange as he tried to take the briefcase away from her. She pushed him away, and he staggered back into the hall.

The chauffeur got into the Jaguar. Dolan ducked his upper body down into the passenger seat as the Jaguar came by, turned into the main street and headed off.

The front door didn't close. There was a shouting match between Julie and Matisse. Julie strode across, got into a battered Futura. Dolan could hear the boy. 'Wait, Wait, bitch! I'm coming.' Matisse ran back into the house.

Julie started the car, reversed it out from the side of the house, turned it. The boy ran out, now shrugged into a huge ex-army coat. He opened the door, fell into the car.

Dolan got his head down again as the Futura came up the broken driveway and past him. He did a quick U-turn, set off medium speed to follow. Hunt's chauffeur at Julie's house paying her off twice the rate for the Markovicz notes. Maybe the explanation for everything included her. He wanted to follow her.

The rain started again. A thin lace of particles that dissolved to smear into the arc of the windscreen wipers. He looked at the gas needle. It was low. Four miles on he saw the first houses of Xavier, still tried to guess at Julie's destination. The Futura took a right. It headed for a large modern factory building. He decided it was probably some silicon software company, like the many now mushrooming up around Napa, attracted by the area of presumed culture, and fine restaurants, spawned by the winemakers and their hordes of visitors.

He decided to risk running into her, turned the car into the front lot of the factory, headed down the side, caught sight of the car a hundred yards away below. Julie's destination had not been the new factory, but another medium-sized building behind it, and fronting on to a parallel road below.

The Futura had turned right, out of a side alley that linked the two buildings, and parked. She and the boy left the car and started a fast walk for an unseen entrance to the lower building. Dolan braked halfway down the alley, got out, strode down to where the Futura was parked. He came round the corner in time to see Matisse consulting a key chain, selecting a key, unlocking a green steel entry door. They both moved inside. Dolan debated his next move. Julie was carrying the briefcase. The door closed. There were no windows on the front façade of the building. There was a small five-foot-high structure on the other side of the door, a pillbox covering over the building's fuel inlet pipes. He walked across, reached the pillbox, moved in behind it.

He did not have to wait long. Four minutes later Matisse reappeared. From his cover Dolan got a good look at the boy's face. Matisse looked terrified, his features distorted by an expression of horror. His face was drained of colour, his eyes goggled, his passage down the steps to the Futura like a creature tranced. In his right hand he carried the briefcase.

Dolan was caught off stroke by the unexpected state of the boy in his reappearance. 'Hey, you, Matisse!'

The boy turned, saw Dolan, and ran. He threw himself and the briefcase into the Futura, slammed the door, locked it, just as Dolan, running fast, reached the door, nearly had his hand pulled off by the sudden powerful take-off of the old car.

Dolan recovered himself, and with a stomach-turning feeling of dread, headed towards the green steel door the fleeing Matisse had left open.

There was a tiny entrance hallway giving on to a large hall. Weak street light coming through the ventilation windows in the hall roof was just enough to penetrate the gloom.

He saw in the hallway a switchbox with its door open. Visible behind the door, a dozen switches. He pressed them all on. Harsh neon flooded the hall beyond the entrance, and, ludicrously, piped Muzak started up.

It was a canning plant. Square in the centre of the huge hall a giant machine consisting of rising flyovers of steel track filled with glinting unlabelled cans. He could see an archway beyond, giving on to other halls. The place was huge. There was a smell of cooked meat.

He moved around the canning machine — no sign

of Julie. He headed across the room and under the first of the archways.

It took little guesswork to recognize this as some kind of kitchen, cooking area. Huge stoves, and vats, and blending machines and racks with ladles and spoons. The floor area was more open here. No sound of movement.

He moved under an arch into the next hall.

Butchers' blocks, a couple of dozen of them, were ranged around two walls to the left and right of the archway. The facing wall had thick, man-high freezer doors set in it, four of them. Julie had described Matisse as a 'butcher'. A butcher in a canning plant? Was this his place of work? The floor was made of steel grid. He could see the steam hoses on the left and right walls, for cleaning the floor.

He found himself for some reason tip-toeing, trying to move softly, but each step a small drum tap on the steel floor.

He walked round a central reservation of more butchers' blocks. He called her name — was shocked himself at the reverberation of sound in the hall, and more, by the alarm in his voice.

He looked at the four freezer doors. He tried the handle of the first one

He pulled open the heavy door. As it opened a light went on inside.

She was sitting, squatting on the floor, covered in blood. It was almost as if she was studying the huge butcher's knife, shaped like a machete, that had been dropped in front of her. The cold room was filled with racks of hanging carcases of beef sides. He stepped, staggered forward, halted. He felt the vomit surge up in his throat.

She had been hit once with the machete knife, from the rear, at neck level. He heard a snap, like a twig breaking. Her spinal cord, half severed, no longer able to support the weight of her head, had snapped. Her head, still held to her shoulders by some skin, fell forward on to her chest.

He stood paralysed, his whole body shaking, some part of his brain dictating flight. She was gone — beyond help. He blundered out of the freezer room, across the butchers' room, and on, searching with his tear-blinded eyes and his shattered, shaking body, for the way out.

A moment later he was standing beside the Hertz car vomiting on to the asphalt.

He got into the car. With hands shaking so badly he had problems getting the ignition key into its lock, he started the motor. He didn't know what to do. The picture of Julie's death scene blinding every sense that could make a decision, blanking his brain.

He slammed the car into gear and drove up past the front factory and slewed the car back on the road to Napa. The car shot up to eighty. There was a red light. He saw it, but for a second couldn't react to it. He slammed on the brakes. The car heeled over and slid, wheels sparking along the curbstones, and then went into a deeper skid as he yanked the wheel to steer again back on to the road. The car mounted the curb and smashed into a brick wall beyond the intersection.

The windscreen caught some projection and shattered in a lacework of tiny fragments over him and into the front compartment of the car. But the car was still driveable, and two minutes later he was at seventy miles an hour again heading for Napa.

Was he injured? He could feel the pain of tiny fragments of glass on his hands and blood slippering the steering wheel. But he didn't stop. He drove faster, the wind tearing straight along the hood and into his eyes, eyes screwed up as he hurled the car up roads, down hills, and into the mist clefts of the valleys. And then through little townships, through cambered curves of streets, past sleeping houses and then finally on to the flat road to Napa. To the north and east a small lake, to the west three lone fir trees, black fingers on a hill. The battered car, urged by him, seemingly as desperate as he, wheeling through corners, tearing at, devouring the miles taking him away from the horror he'd found in the dark building.

One mile north of Napa, where the road widens to sweep under trees, he slammed on the brakes and brought the car to a halt. He sat back, switched on the interior lights, twisted the car mirror and studied his blanched face and bleeding fingers. He took out a cigarette, his hands shaking so badly that he could hardly light it. And then he had to throw it away almost immediately because he was crying silently, the helpless, bottomless tears like a child weeps, were coursing down his cheeks.

Later, he found a phone kiosk, telephoned Beverly Hills Police, left a detailed message for Hagen, then phoned the Napa Police.

Napa Central P.D. boasted three officers and two burly detectives, men who listened rather than led the conversation, both with the disconcerting habit of standing up, with Dolan in mid-sentence, and going off to make a phone call about the pursuit of Matisse, or the formulation of a ten-man murder squad.

Dolan told them an outline — no mention of his identifying Hunt's chauffeur, just a chauffeur. And saying the victim had said to him that she was getting a large sum of cash from an undisclosed source — presumably the contents of the briefcase.

Hagen phoned, talked to the cops and said he would be in Napa as near to seven as he could make it.

The detectives seemed mollified by the Hagen call — their intuition telling them that they were not getting the full story from Dolan. The taller of the two, around four a.m., asked Dolan where he was staying. Would he be going back to his ex-wife's house? Dolan said he'd be happy to sleep a few hours in a police cell. Clearly they didn't want him wandering, and agreed. They took six cushions off some chairs and he stretched out in a cell. Surprised, he found himself falling asleep, his mind too confused and shattered to race any thoughts that could start calculating any conclusions.

Hagen woke him up. He had a cup of boiling black coffee in each hand.

Dolan groaned into an upright position on the cold slat bench. His restless sleep had pushed the cushions off. He'd slept on the bare bench.

'Where do we talk? Here?' Hagen asked quietly.

'Here.'

Hagen sat down, handed the second cup of coffee to Dolan. 'I'll give it to you simple, and all of it's the facts — true. Let me run through it before your questions.' He sipped the coffee, grimaced at its heat. 'I don't know anything more than you about this Leon Markovicz. Not one fact more than you give me. All I know is he upset a lot of people — I mean, Defence people, Army people. As you know, I have my name as a contact to you on your file. So some big-wig from United States Army Intelligence comes to me and says, "You know J. Dolan, do us a favour, put him together with this guy Stone, and see if you can set him up with this girl, Christa Beecham". And he talked to my chief. My chief ordered me to do these things. Don't ask me what the fuck Army Intelligence has to do with anything. I know nothing at all about U.S. Army Intelligence and its activities.' He paused. 'Bear with me.'

'Just keep to the truth.' Dolan's voice was cold.

'Okay. So I agree to set you up. Because I want to know why — for you. I'm not that keen on my department, John. I find out this Stone guy has links to organized crime. So I tell you. That's it. Now what about your ex-wife?'

Dolan told him about the phone call, the hundred thousand supposed to be arriving in cash. Hunt's chauffeur, the crazy kid, a 'butcher' by trade, the drive to the slaughterhouse. His idea that the boy had killed her, stolen the money.

'Okay.' Hagen pursed his lips. 'You may have it right. I'll personally check Hunt and the hundred grand — see if he'll talk about it. You got the address?'

Dolan told Hagen the address.

'You think I should do that?'

'Yes.'

'One last thing. I got something for you.' Hagen started fishing in his wallet. 'Remember I went to City Hall, see if anything had turned up there for incorporation in the probate of Markovicz' estate?'

'Yes?'

'When I left the Civic Legal Department, I told 'em to pass on anything that did come in for the probate.'

'Yes?'

'You said Markovicz had a big grey truck?'

'Yes?'

'A bill from a camp site at Colleano Beach for rent of a truck space.' He handed the invoice across to Dolan.

The invoice was headed, 'North Colleano Leisure Sites Inc.' It was a bill for forty-eight dollars for six weeks' parking. In handwriting on the bottom of the bill, a message. 'This is a leisure park. Your truck is unsightly and we request you move it to extreme end of park and not in future park it among the holiday and residential campers.'

* * *

He arrived back at L.A. International at eleven a.m. He found a phone booth, dialled Christa's number. Colville answered. 'Dolan.'

There was the sound of the receiver of the name catching his breath. Then a pause. Then, stonily, 'What d'you want?'

'I've found the grey trailer. Markovicz's.'

'Where?' The excitement of the man made him almost bark the word into the phone.

'Jesus, d'you think I'd tell you?'

'I'm on your side, John.'

'Shit you. And whose side are you on?'

'Don't be crass.'

'Sure. You may have heard from your fellow conspirators. Julie's dead. Murdered. Mrs Markovicz's dead.'

There was horror in Colville's voice. 'Julie! Murdered?!'

'I'm coming now to you. If I smell cops, or government officials, or organized crime, or Christ Jesus knows what else, at or around your place, anything suspicious, I'll drive on.'

'You'll take me to the trailer?'

'Fuck you.'

'I'll be waiting.'

'Is Christa there?' Dolan added.

'Yes.'

'She comes too. I'll be half an hour.'

He was beyond noticing the strain, caring about her feelings, Christa's. She tried to ask him about Julie, the death, and its circumstances. He cut her short. The only surprise to him was that they didn't know — a bunch of lousy, lying conspirators, and they were all maybe cheating and holding back from each other.

He'd arrived at the front door of the Laurel Canyon

house just after noon. Colville and Christa were waiting poised in the hall.

'Where are we going? Where's the Markovicz truck?'

'Colville, you follow me.'

'Are we going to it?' Colville had an edge of contempt in the sharpness of his question, as if he felt Dolan was about to waste his time.

'We're going. We take two cars. You follow me. Christa comes with me. If I find we're being followed, I'll lead you to Disneyland and you can shove your head up Donald Duck's ass.'

'Why are you taking us to Markovicz' truck?'

'Because I can guess at the desperation, you bastard. You really want to see that truck.'

They went out to the cars. Dolan consulted his route map again. He started the Chrysler, gave the map to Christa, and said, 'Get us to Englefield.'

'It's easy from here. Is the truck at Englefield?'

'No, it isn't.'

He drove off down the steep road to Sunset. A grimfaced Colville in his Ford Limited followed.

She made one piece of conversation on the hour-drive to Englefield. 'I really loved you, John, the day in Arrowhead. When this is over . . . Dennis and me, we may not last together . . . it's at the point of habit. Four years together. When this is over . . .'

'When what is over?'

She had no answer. She went back to the route again, with clipped messages navigated him across town and south-west to the ocean.

'Wait in the car,' Colville ordered Christa. He'd got out of the Ford Limited, crossed to the parked Chrysler. Dolan was out of the Chrysler. Christa was getting out. She sat back in the car.

'This is it?' Colville looked tired by the journey,

asked the question as if he didn't really want confirmation, just a brief nod and on with investigating the long grey trailer.

Dolan ignored him. He was orienting himself to the layout of the beach site. There were forty to fifty campers and caravans parked in a radius, with a small site service cabin in the centre. Above the service cabin a hoarding in faded paint, 'North Colleano Leisure Sites Inc.'

The sound of the sea the only intrusion on the silence. The beach site made a gentle slope down to the ocean two hundred yards away. In summer the place might be thronged by people, barracked by the noise of children. But the cold breeze from the water, now choppy in its winter guise, had expelled people back to the city. Dolan searched the lines of campers for any sign of human life. There was no movement.

Colville had walked across to the grey truck, stood up on its driver's side, tried the driver's door. It was locked. He moved on to the rear of the truck. He called back, 'Hey, Dolan. The whole rear of this truck is welded closed. And reinforced strips welded across. Leon didn't intend anybody getting in.'

'The entrance must be from the driver's cab.'

'Driver's door's locked.'

'I'll deal with it.' Dolan turned to Christa. 'Maybe you should stay put.' He raised his voice again to Colville. 'I'll get something.'

'This is primer black over a kind of leaded surface. Lead.' Colville indicated the exterior of the truck. Dolan didn't get the significance and wasn't sure Colville was making an important point. He moved around to the trunk of the Chrysler, opened it, and took out a wheel brace. He walked across the sand to Colville at the truck. He got up on the step, and hit the driver's side window with the wheel brace.

'Jesus. Hey! Can we do this? Listen, I don't want to know law breaking,' Colville protested.

'It's down to me.' Dolan reached in through the shattered glass and unlocked and opened the door. He stepped into the cab.

Colville stood there, still hesitant, waiting for the sound of possible enquiry, a shout nearby to signal that the smashing of the glass had raised attention. The trailers around slept on like tombs. Nothing, no movement, except the low clouds shadowing in from the ocean.

'There's a door here.' Dolan meant a door from the driver's cab into the truck section. 'Come on.' This said with an edge of command in case Colville might be defining the reconnaissance as optional.

'I'm behind you.' Colville climbed into the cab.

A small steel door led from the driver's compartment into the rear. Dolan had the door open, was standing stooped in the doorway, looking into the darkened space.

'You want a match?'.

Dolan already had a book of matches out. He started fumbling with it, finally got one alight. He saw something high on the wall. 'Maybe a light switch.' He pressed it.

Slowly a weak baleful light flickered on from two overhead strips of neon. Colville followed Dolan into the compartment.

It was a rough square. Its two side walls were stacked with equipment up to the ceiling of the truck. The equipment was on shelves of slotted steel angle. Dolan noticed the odd assortment of bolts, some too long, some with missing nuts, some rusty, that had been used in creating the shelving. An amateur had put this together.

There was a sheet steel wall at the other end of the cubicle. It had a door set in it. Near the top of the door a circular glass peephole framed in brass. Dolan moved to the peephole, looked through it, could see nothing in the blackness beyond.

'Let me see.' Colville was at his shoulder. Dolan angled himself sideways in the constricted space. Colville put his eye to the peephole.

'Okay, we have this cubicle, roughly eight feet long. Through there another cubicle, must be about ten feet long. Yale lock. Should be breakable. Now what is all this stuff? Oxygen? Nitrogen?' Dolan was pointing out the cylinders strapped to the steel shelving.

'It's a controlled environment. Not here, but in there.' Colville pointed at the steel door. 'All this is providing a sealed, controlled, filtered, heated atmosphere for the space in there.'

'Air-conditioning equipment?'

'It's a bit more sophisticated than that. If this truck is Leon's secret, this is not the important end of it. It's in there.' Colville's eye was pressed against the peephole. He started to strike some matches, and angle them against the glass. 'Can't make it out. Can't see a thing.'

Dolan pushed him aside.

'I'm going to open this.'

'No.' Colville sounded worried.

'Get out of my way.' There was a tyre lever built into the handle end of the wheel brace. Dolan now attacked the edge of the door around the lock area. The tyre lever edge wouldn't fit into the gap.

'You won't open it that way. It's solid, designed to seal airtight.' Colville now wriggled past Dolan, and turned his attention to the stacked equipment again, instruments, dials, coils, tubing, cylinders, mechanical and electrical components.

Dolan pushed past Colville. 'Don't move from here.'

'What are you doing?'

'I'll get a rock from the beach, hit the door. Maybe distort the edge so I can get the tyre lever in.'

'Why don't we get some outside help? A locksmith? I'll go try and find one.'

'You're not leaving here,' Dolan commanded.

'Jesus.' Colville's eyes were now scrutinizing the counter dial. 'There's radium here. Christ!' He had turned, excited and alarmed. A cylindrical stainless steel tank, two feet in diameter, was metal-strapped to some shelving at the side. 'Jesus, d'you know how much radium must be in here in a tank this size?!'

Dolan studied the scientist, his anguish and confusion.

'D'you understand?' Colville wasn't looking at him, but now more intently at the instruments lined away from the cylindrical container.

'Shit. Understand what?'

'Radium. No private individual is allowed to have it. Leon must have stolen . . . fucking crazy.' He switched his alarm into a look that seemed to be accusing Dolan. 'Jesus.' He swore again. 'I got to do something about this.' And he made a sudden movement to push past.

Dolan's voice was hard. 'You hold it.' He was angry, near defeated. 'I lost my wife, murdered. I've been lied to, conspired against, humiliated, and now, this moment, I need to know. What is all this? I think you know. You're going to . . .'

' . . .Your guess is as good as mine!'

'You're lying!'

'Why the shit would I lie?'

'There may be a flashlight in the Chrysler. Don't you move.' The violence of Dolan's instruction made Colville take a step back.

Dolan moved to the door into the front cab, swung his legs through the driver's and passenger's seats, clambered out into the grey day, and down on to the sand.

He paced to the Chrysler. Christa opened the passenger door, started to get out. 'No, stay put,' he said sharply.

'What have you found?'

'Nothing.' He reached in and pulled down the glove pocket. There was a flashlight inside. He pulled it out, switched it on. No light. The batteries flat.

'What d'you want?'

'We're trying to see into a compartment.'

'I've got a Zippo lighter.' She reached into the pocket of her bag.

He took the lighter and headed back for the truck.

He lost his footing on the driver's step, slipped, recovered himself, swung himself up into the cab, took a step towards the door into the long cab.

Corville's skull came out like a bullet. His forehead smashed straight into Dolan's face. Dolan let out a noise, half scream of pain, half expletive, and crashed backwards, unbalanced, the full weight of his body hitting the windscreen. He rolled sideways, groaned again as the blunt hard knob of the gear shift knifed into his side. All he saw as he grabbed for Colville was the man's legs. But he couldn't get a hold. And Colville was out, almost head first, through the driver's door, to crash on to the sand below.

And then Colville was running like something demented for the Ford Limited.

Dolan, creased double with pain, managed to get his body, with flailing hands and legs, upright. He took two pain-seared steps towards following Colville out, and stopped.

Colville had reached his car, pulled open the driver's door, fallen into it and started it, in one continuous series of actions. Sand spewed up in the air as Colville hit the accelerator and turned the car slewing and bumping across the beach and away towards the entry road. In seconds he was gone from sight.

Christa was out of the Chrysler. 'What is it? Where's he gone? What's happening?!'

'Just stay there!' He shouted at her, through lips which were spilling blood from the wounds caused by Colville's head. 'You may have to get help. But wait! Stay with the car!'

She said something, but he didn't hear. He was striding back up and slightly away from the grey truck, towards a pile of garbage. By the pile a piece of rock, twenty or thirty pounds weight. He lifted it, eyes still bleared with tears, blood still pouring from his nose down on to his arms. He staggered with the rock back to the truck.

'I told you, get back! Stay in the car with the engine running.' As he clambered into the cab he saw her, this time, doing as instructed.

He stepped into the first cubicle, and moved down to the door.

He examined the door area around the lock again, worked out the feasibility of hitting the steel plate hard enough to bend it, distort it enough to get the tyre lever in, and wrench the lock. He raised the stone and slammed it hard against the lock. The rock bounced on contact. He cursed. The door was too solidly made.

He changed his mind. It was possible that the Yale lock had a handle on the other side. He angled the rock round to a pointed end, and aimed it sharply straight at the glass window peephole. The glass disintegrated with a noise like a pistol shot.

He pulled his denim jacket sleeve up and fed his hand slowly through the peephole. His hand went down. A second of triumph. There was a handle behind the Yale lock. He turned it and pulled outwards. The door opened.

Behind the door a glass wall, with a glass door set in it. There was a handle on the glass door, but no lock. He flicked the Zippo lighter. There was a light switch, just inside to the left of the outer steel door. He switched on the light. It was a similar arrangement to the first cubicle — two strips of overhead neon blinked on in the cubicle behind the glass. He took stock. An outer steel wall with an inner glass wall, a locked door on the steel wall, a handle but apparently no lock on the glass door. In the cubicle beyond, a table piled high with equipment, including a small cassette recorder, and more steel shelving and equipment round the walls.

He opened the glass door, stepped into the cubicle. He let out an oath. Something had exploded behind him. He took an involuntary further step into the cubicle, looked back at the door. The door had slammed closed and relocked itself.

He stepped back to the door. No handle on this side. He could see the mechanism that had closed it. It was a stainless steel fitting, smooth on the outside. It was a substantial lock. He spun round at the sound of Leon Markovicz' voice. It was coming from the cassette recorder. He stood stock still in shock for a moment, and then moved towards it, saw the wires leading from the machine to the door. It had been switched on by the action of opening the door.

Markovicz' voice was low, almost a whisper. 'This is your madness, not mine. I take it the intruder into this cubicle is a scientist, perhaps an ex-colleague. Do nothing for a moment, but listen.'

Dolan picked up the cassette player, turned up the volume. 'You've been brought here by the police who have found this trailer — the police, handmaidens to our mad rulers,' the voice continued. 'You've just come through an airlock. I'm mechanical. I'm competent. It took me a long time to build this trap.' Dolan put down the recorder, then stood still. The voice of the dead man had ordered him to do nothing. He could think of nothing to do for the moment but listen. 'I hope the sequences function as I designed and constructed them. You've walked through an armoured glass door. It's relocked. You can smash at it with your fists or with any solid item I've left in this cubicle. But you'll find it's impossible to break armoured glass. And in a minute from now, you'll listen, you'll realize you can't, you must never, smash the glass.'

On the sound track Dolan could hear the rustle of papers. Markovicz was obviously reading from a prepared text. 'This is my laboratory. Within this small place I did my work, when I was exiled by my colleagues. I worked here for a year. Then I spent more time, turning it into a trap. You know what my work was? Phylloxera, the tiny louse, no bigger than a pin head, with its lunatic pace of reproduction. Twenty-five million eggs a year. Normally to attack vines, as at the end of the last century. But there are certain hybrids which behave differently. I discovered these hybrids. I discovered a species of phyllox that attacked basic crops. I discovered a method of cloning them. I investigated this area for preventive purposes. My discoveries frightened me. I wanted others to see the danger. Then, sinisterly, I found certain colleagues of mine were co-opting my work, and being paid by government to develop it. The "Silent Soldier" project. The soldier the size of a pin head who is placed in the fields of our enemy to destroy his harvests, his foodstuffs.'

He heard Markovicz sigh, a low shuddering intake. He'd heard that sigh many times over the years of their friendship. 'I can imagine the event that sparked the decision to pursue the "Silent Soldier" project. It would have been a few years back — when the Russians came cap in hand to buy American grain. Yes, they needed grain, and someone amongst you scientists, or rulers, must have had the thought – "What if they had no grain at all?" That's how your minds work. This is how my mind could never work. I told you, all of you, that you were working on the deadliest weapon in history. For this you persecuted me, exiled me, drove me to death. I've spent my life fighting against the Hitlers in government and science. This cubicle is the legacy. Don't try to break down the glass door. Do as I tell you. Look on this table. There's a two-way radio – a walkie-talkie. There's another one in the cubicle outside.'

Dolan could see the small flat two-way radio. He picked it up. 'Press the transmit button. Your colleagues who will come here can listen to you and this recording. This is my message.'

Dolan turned over the two-way radio. There was a transmit button, and an amplifier slide. 'The sequence is: you entered the door. An explosive device relocked it. The same explosive charge triggered the opening of the red-framed glass case. It's on the shelf to the left of the glass door. The case was pressurized. In the air now, millions of them, millions of genetically engineered and cloned phylloxera. Can you see them? The form they'll take is a kind of haze, a mist . . .'

He couldn't see anything. Then he looked down at the floor. There was a haze, like floating particles of brown flour, just above floor level.

'So you wanted to engineer billions of phyllox to attack the grain belts of your enemy. You were to engineer and clone only the male phylloxera with their life cycle of two years. It would destroy, but not reproduce. The phylloxera in this cubicle are both male and female. If they are freed, their life cycle will last until they have destroyed all the food resources of the world. But that's the point. They won't get out. And you won't get out.'

Dolan was concentrating on the voice – it seemed to be the first time he had heard Markovicz articulate so carefully, easily. It was as if the entire confusion of the man's life had been a process of sorting out one final, simple, and horrific message.

'This is what will happen. You will die in here. I have given you enough oxygen for some hours. But your colleagues can add more oxygen through the boost supply from the second cabin - if they dare to take the risk. If you receive more oxygen, then you will die of starvation. The lice will die, I calculate, in two or three months – from starvation. They need only microns of oxygen. The scientists who dared to think of developing this weapon will sit outside the glass door and watch you die. D'you get the point of it? The reason for this trap? Let me spell it out. For the last several decades the madmen of government, and the scientific establishment, have not only approved, but heaped honours on those so-called scientists who dared to work towards the destruction of our species. Whether it was Oppenheimer or Edward Teller and their fission bombs, or the Dow Chemical scientists inventing napalm, or "yellow rain". It has become an accepted fact, an approved avocation, that a scientist may use his God-given gifts on the destruction of his fellow man. This trap is designed to bring every scientist in the world up short in his tracks. I want you all to watch one of your own people die. Why? Because it was always others who perished. I believe the man in this trap worked on the "Silent Soldier" project – this vilest of weapons. I want scientists everywhere to witness a scientist's death, in this cubicle, surrounded by millions of tiny phylloxera who, were they released, could destroy the foodcrops of the world. I've even arranged that this death cell is on four wheels – so you can tour around the great universities and seats of learning. "The Dying Scientist Show". Yes, drive this truck to Berkeley, to M.I.T. This has got to be the only way to bring home to scientists, and the Hitlers, your rulers, the consequences of all insane research.'

For a few seconds Dolan wasn't sure whether the message was over. The small hum from the cassette a neutral background to his mind racing, trying to think back to Markovicz' lectures on the great root pest, the tiny louse that had originated in America, and gone on to devastate all the European vineyards in the late part of the last century. Now, according to Markovicz, the lice could be genetically engineered, cloned from a pest into a weapon. He saw the madman's logic of it. A scientist, sealed in a glass-fronted cage which could never be unsealed, watched by his fellow scientists as he succumbed to starvation, or suffocation. The only thing the madman had miscalculated was that he might trap the wrong man.

He picked up the two-way radio, pressed the transmit button, and shouted into it, 'Christa! Christa!' He quickly put it down. He was sure that the volume of the receiver, wherever it was, and if it was actuated by the transmit button, would probably not reach outside the truck.

No one entered from the cab.

He got down on his knees. He examined the floating cloud of brown specks settling into a film on the floor. He saw they were on his hands, and that a film of brown was tracing down the uprights on the shelves. He shuddered, got up, moved fast around the table examining the shelves. He was looking for something to smash at the glass door or wall, and yet he knew he couldn't do that, not yet. He had to get a grip of himself and try to make some sense of Markovicz' words - the possibility that the man had miscalculated, that this was some kind of fantasy joke. But his knowledge of the man ruled this out.

He stood still examining the various items of heavier equipment on the rear shelves. He spun around. About five minutes had passed since Colville had butted him in the face. He could feel the vibration of heavy footsteps from up front, from somebody clambering into the truck. And then suddenly Colville was coming through from the driver's cab. Behind Colville, two uniformed cops, large men. The narrow passage between the shelving outside filled by the three men.

Colville came straight at the glass door, pushed it, then started to apply his shoulder. Dolan grabbed up the two-way radio. 'Dennis. Stop! Stop! Can you hear me?'

He saw Colville's head turn, his eyes searching the second shelf to his left. Then Colville took up the small flat box with its tiny aerial.

'There's a message on the tape in here, from Leon.' Dolan indicated the tape recorder. 'Listen to it. I'll rewind it. Don't do anything until you've heard it.'

Dolan pressed the rewind button, groaned in fury at the slow speed of the rewind. Finally the button came up. He pressed 'play' and placed the speaker of the cassette recorder on the table next to the walkie-talkie.

For the twenty seconds of the opening paragraphs of the tape, he watched Colville's face, studied the colour draining from it. Then he turned away. If he was going to get out of here, it would be through his own efforts – Colville was enemy. A cubicle piled high with equipment. There must be something, some item, some chemistry, some wherewithal, to probe and find a flaw in Leon's trap. His eyes searching again the slotted steel shelving. Electrical, mechanical, and laboratory equipment. It made no sense – it related to nothing in his experience. This pile of retorts, machinery, gas bottles, ducting, wiring, was a world away from the guttural drone of Markovicz lecturing in an almost empty classroom years ago. The playback was concluding.

'Hey, Colville!' Dolan shouted down the mike as the recording finished. 'What d'you think?'

'It's . . . it's . . . For Christ's sake, don't attempt to get out. We'll think of something.'

'Will you?' Dolan didn't like the edge of panic in the man's voice. 'What are the two cops for?'

'Dolan, listen.' Colville was pressing the transmit button.

'I can hear you.'

'Look, these cops, and other people, have been following us. I had a direction bleeper in my car. I and others – we've been looking for this truck – knew it contained Leon's laboratory. Knew it would be a significant discovery. But we had no idea he'd organized this. The important thing is not to do anything precipitous.'

'No, I'll just sit around here, starve to death, suffocate.' Dolan edged the sarcasm with threat. 'Is that what you think I'm going to do?'

'What can I say?'

'Say something, Dennis. Like say whether you were on the "Silent Soldier" project.'

The shift in Colville's eyes was enough of an answer.

'There's equipment in here, heavy equipment. I think I'll try smashing it against the glass, test Leon's calculation about how tough it is.'

'For Christ's sake!' Colville's voice was shocked, impotent.

'I'm running this show, Dennis.'

'People are on the way. Experts.'

'Never mind about that. You do this for me, now. Bring two people here. One is a guy called Reuben Weiss, Reuben's Wine Store, Encino. Phylloxera was called the Bordeaux Blight. You're just a fucking scientist. I want a wine expert. 1144 Jason Avenue, Encino. Get him now. Do it!'

He saw Colville on the other side of the glass turn to one of the cops and talk to him.

'I also want Detective Don Hagen, Beverly Hills P.D. You get them here fast. Or I break the glass.'

'Jesus, Dolan. You got to take it easy. You don't know what you're saying.'

'I know exactly what I'm saying. The irony of panic, Dennis, is that a person's instinct is to rush a lot of decisions, when he should be taking it slow. I know that, Dennis. I'll be taking it careful. But you're going to do exactly what I say. Get Reuben and Hagen.'

Colville was now remonstrating with the cop, who obviously had instructions to stay put. Dolan could hear some of the words. 'Go. The guy's crazy. I know him.' It was as if Colville didn't care that Dolan could hear him on the radio. One of the cops turned and lumbered out of the second cubicle.

'I want you to do this now, John. I want you to move down each shelf and describe in detail the equipment. Take, it slow. Give me every detail – any markings on the equipment.'

'Why?'

'It looks like we can't get in to you. There may be something in there, something you can use to get out. I see gas bottles. I see apparatus. I want to know what it is. I'm going to take notes. I'll get some paper.'

* * *

And Colville was gone, and Dolan was staring at the second cop. The cop stared back through a pair of rimless glasses. His face was impassive, a mask.

Colville was back a minute later. 'Okay,' he said into the radio. 'I'm going to make a map of everything in your cubicle. Start at the top right, by the door. What's there?'

'Nothing.'

'Jesus, Dolan, get it right! This side there's a bimetal tube from a cylinder here, entering into your cubicle. D'you see a tube?'

'Right.'

'Where does it lead?'

'Along here to another cylinder.'

'Any markings on the cylinder?'

'A.O.L., then a dozen digits, and letters, on a metal strap.'

'That's your oxygen supply. Read out the digits and letters.'

Dolan read out the line of letters and figures.

'Go on. Go back to the corner by the door. Start on the top shelf. Describe what's there.'

'There's a kind of glass jar.'

'Sealed?'

'Right. Two tubes into its top. There's a liquid inside.'

'Colour?'

'Green. Colville, any point in this?'

'For Christ's sake, keep going.'

Dolan went on. There were six shelves, each crammed with apparatus. Colville took down the descriptions, asked questions in a voice getting terser and more demanding. Dolan was looking at his watch. He calculated that there'd been twenty minutes of descriptions when the tall man walked in.

The man had a military coat over an army uniform.

He was in his fifties. He moved in, squeezing past the cop with the rimless glasses. He touched Colville's shoulder. Colville spun round. Dolan heard the instruction on the walkie-talkie. 'Come with me,' the tall man ordered. 'You know who I am?'

'Yes, sir. But I've got to finish this. And we can't leave him alone.'

'Come with me.' The words now colder.

'Dolan, I'll be back. Don't do anything. Nothing. D'you understand?'

Dolan looked at the agitated scientist. He didn't bother to reply.

They were gone five minutes. Dolan occupied his time, trying to run his own check. Colville had said there might be something to attack chemically, or burn, or somehow destroy the parasites. But Leon would have thought of this – would have calculated this reponse. The only entry into this cubicle seemed to be the oxygen tube. By angling his body hard against the glass partition near the door, he could see the oxygen tank in the first compartment. The two cylinders were small. He'd tried scuba diving years before. They looked like cylinders from scuba diving gear.

Then Colville and the man in army uniform were back. And Colville was pointing up at the first oxygen cylinder. But the walkie-talkie had been switched off by the army man, and Dolan couldn't hear what was said.

Dolan rapped sharply on the glass partition – pointed at the walkie-talkie the army man had placed on a shelf. The man picked it up, pressed the transmit switch. 'Yes?'

'Leave the two-way on. I want to hear what you're saying.'

'Understood.'

'What are you doing?'

‘People are arriving. We’re doing our best.’

‘I want Reuben Weiss.’

‘He’ll be here in five minutes.’

Dolan did some quick mental arithmetic, twenty minutes of describing the interior of the cubicle to Colville, four minutes’ absence of Colville and the military guy, plus five minutes. ‘Don’t lie to me. How could you get him from Encino to here so fast?’

‘Police helicopter in Encino has picked him up.’ The army man turned to Colville. ‘Get out,’ he said, flatly, curt, matter-of-fact.

Colville said nothing, turned and moved past the tall man and out to the cab.

‘I’m Aldin.’ The man’s voice was low, with a New England accent. ‘You’re in a sealed capsule and that’s the way it’s got to stay. There’s one entrance point only into the capsule. This boost supply oxygen entry. But can we tamper with it? Can we take the risk?’

‘I’ll let you know. I’ll give you maybe a chance to work some way round this. Then I’m coming out.’

‘You’re not coming out, Mr Dolan, believe me. You’re not leaving this truck alive, unless we allow you to. So no more threats. And just do exactly what you’re told. What’s involved here is something with greater potential for destruction than nuclear fission. It’s an obscenity, worked out by a genius, the same genius who’s constructed this trap.’

The cop with the rimless glasses had entered again. He approached the military man. Dolan heard the announcement. ‘Senator Towers has arrived. And the Berkeley people.’

‘Right,’ Aldin responded. He turned to Dolan. ‘I’m asking you to sit it out for a few minutes until we get some expert opinions. One of the things we’re going to have to do is move this truck, tow it, down the park into a more open area. You’d better sit down during the tow. Okay?’

'You. You've got a limited time, then I will do something.'

Aldin didn't respond. He pushed past the cop with the rimless glasses and on out of the cab.

Dolan moved back to the shelves. He could see some calculation upcoming from Aldin and others which would rid them of the cubicle, but with himself still inside. There was a solid-looking transformer, a ten-pounder bunch of metal, secured by two bolts to one shelf. The bolts had been put on loosely. He started to unscrew them. The first one came easily. The second was stiff.

He heard the sound of a steel wire tow rope being fixed to the rear of the chassis. Now there was a jerk, and he nearly lost balance. The truck rolled, yawing gently along on its tow backwards across the soft sand. The motion ceased. Dolan returned to the recalcitrant second nut on the transformer.

He heard his name called over the radio.

'John.' Aldin was back. Reuben was with him. It was such a familiar face, so wreathed in perplexity, that Dolan almost laughed. Aldin handed the fat little man the walkie-talkie.

'Jesus, John, they dropped a helicopter right in the street outside the store. And I'm grabbed, thrown in like crap. What the shit's going on? What the hell is this?' Reuben's fat face was always covered in sweat. Now he had a fistful of kleenex, was wiping forehead, face and neck as he talked. 'I was kidnapped, for Christ's sake! I swore on my mother's grave I would never fly in a helicopter. You'd better have a real good story for this. You know, to me, you're a guy who kicks me a few cases of wine. I never want hassle from cops or anyone.'

'Reuben,' Dolan said gently. 'We have to talk.'

'There's cops outside, helicopters, guys in fire suits. What d'you want from me, John? What's happening?' The kleenex was still dabbing feverishly around the man's face.

'There are experts coming here trying to deal with a problem I've got in this cubicle. They're scientists. You're a different expert. You know about wine. You've got to talk to me about the Bordeaux Blight . . .'

'You're kidding?' The little man was looking wide-eyed.

'No. You've been brought here to talk to me, and this guy, about phylloxera, the great Bordeaux Blight. Now no shit, no bluster. No panic. Take it easy. Search back in your memory. Give me all the facts you know. I studied the botany of it. What about the history of it? Just talk. Tell me and him, about phylloxera. And do it now. Right?'

Something of the edge in Dolan's voice had got through to the little man. He had calmed.

'Go on, Reuben.'

'What d'you want to know?'

'Start at the beginning. The beginning of the blight. What were the dates?'

'It struck Bordeaux, 1880s, 1890s.'

'I remember something happened — it came in two surges. Each time there was a period when the blight was curtailed . . .'

'Jesus, they replanted all the vines with resistant stock.'

'No, before that, before the replanting.'

'Are you kidding me?'

'Reuben, listen. Before the replanting . . .The disease reached a zenith, and then it remitted. Some châteaux survived without replanting — well, at least for a time. Come on, Reuben!' Dolan said sharply, as if he felt the man's panic, disorientation, was confusing him, and he needed a sharp word to bring him down to earth.

'I still don't know what you want.' The little man had turned to Aldin, some calculation that Aldin represented sanity, and authority.

'Answer him,' Aldin said coldly.

Reuben wiped his neck. 'March 1885, heavy storms in Bordeaux and Burgundy. April 1897, wind — hail, wiped out Romanee Conti, Beaujolais. Also terrible weather in Bordeaux . . .'

'Why did it affect the phyllox?' Aldin cut in.

'Jesus, I don't know if it did affect the phyllox! Listen, the guy we need to talk to is Dave Weitzelman. He's got that encyclopaedic brain of crap about early Bordeaux vintages.'

'Aldin. You hear me?'

Aldin stepped around Reuben, took the two-way from him. 'Yes.'

'Listen. Can you rig up a telephone in here so Reuben and me can talk to a guy in Sonoma? Also, Reuben, there's Charles Leacock in Napa — the librarian.'

'Sure, he knows his wine.' Reuben was nodding.

'All right, how many phones?' Aldin asked tersely.

'That's it,' Dolan said. 'Weitzelman in Sonoma, Leacock in Napa.'

'I can bring in two field telephones which we can shortwave into Bell,' Aldin offered.

'Two phones then. And, Aldin, there's a transformer — a bunch of heavy metal. If I run low on oxygen I'm going to smash the glass.'

'Don't,' Aldin said it flatly. He turned and moved fast out to the front of the trailer.

'Well shit, John, what the fuck's going on here?'

'Be quiet a minute, Reuben,' Dolan ordered.

'You can't do this to me, John. Haul me in here, tell me to shut my mouth.'

Dolan tried to make the explanation simple. He found himself describing Markovicz as a 'madman'.

He told Reuben the scientist had built a trap. It was supposed to have caught a fellow scientist. The madman was trying to make some point about scientists and destruction. He had the impression that Reuben was still too confused to take most of it in. Ten minutes passed, then Aldin reappeared with two guys in military uniforms, both sergeants. Khaki-coloured field telephones were set up on a shelf. Aldin asked Reuben for the names again — spoke into one of the field telephones asking some Bell operator to find the numbers.

Dolan checked the glass door again. The explosive bolt had no nuts, screws, on its surface — no obvious way of dismantling it. He sat down, tried to think of the questions he would ask Weitzelman and Leacock. Weitzelman, a young guy with forty hectares in Sonoma, making one of the best Cabernet Sauvignons. Weitzelman spent all day in the vineyard, all night in his study reading about wine. Then late night making kids with his wife. He had five kids. Lena Weitzelman was always toting a babe around in her arms. Leacock was chief librarian of the Napa Wine Institute Library. Another young guy, completely bald, brilliant, antisocial. It had taken years for Dolan to get to know him.

Aldin was ringing the numbers now on both telephones. Each phone was sitting on an Amplivox cradle. Aldin turned to Dolan and gave a brief nod, then repositioned the two-way radio next to the phones.

Dolan took up the two-way, pressed the transmit button. 'David, Charles, this is John Dolan. I have Reuben Weiss here. And we have a problem. When you speak, you'll have to speak up. We're going to try and conduct a four-way conversation via amplified phones. Do you hear me?'

He heard the assents of the two men from the telephones.

'It's going to be impossible to explain in detail my situation. I've got mixed up in a lab experiment to do with engineering the bug phylloxera. We're in a mess. We need urgently, not scientific information about the bug, but some history of the phyllox outbreaks in Bordeaux . . .'

Suddenly Dolan caught and interpreted Aldin's expression. Aldin was looking from himself to Reuben. It was almost as if the army man was sneering at them — he'd solved the problem for the moment, of keeping Dolan involved and inside the glass trap. He'd proven Dolan could be dictated to. 'Hey, Aldin, get out of here. You're part of them, the establishment, the scientists. Leave this truck. It's over to us, the wine lovers . . . Get out, now!'

Aldin didn't say anything. He turned and moved out.

'What's going on?' Leacock had heard the bawled order.

'Listen to me, both of you. Charles, phylloxera — the history. Reuben says it struck, 1880s, 1890s.'

'Okay, you want a precise date? First sign of phyllox, 1881. March. The flowering,' Leacock offered.

'It's always about the flowering that the vine begins to succumb,' Dave Weitzelman added.

'I want to know about the remission. The disease waned twice — is that right?' Dolan asked.

'Yeah,' Leacock's voice agreed. 'After 1885 and 1897.'

'This is the question. Why did it wane? Why did the plague succumb for a while, on two occasions, before it was rooted out by replanting?'

'You people keep talking. I'm in the wine library. I've just been working with Lotbinière's diary. It's got a lot of weather detail,' Leacock said.

'John, are you hearing me?' Weitzelman asked.

'Yes.'

'Well, the two dates are maybe significant because of the weather disasters. Both vintages were largely destroyed by major storms. And there was frost as well at each flowering.'

'That's what Reuben says. Reuben remembered the storms.'

'Right,' Reuben was nodding.

'The question is why?' Dolan persisted. 'If the frost caused the remission, how much frost was there?'

'Listen,' Leacock was back at the phone. 'When you talked about remission after 1885, 1897, it looked to me that it might be the weather. I've got de Lotbinière's "Journal" here, the archive of Château Chalon. I'm looking quickly at the vintage 1885. There's something here. It snowed. "Snow on the ground for a week at the flowering. The considerable showers melted causing the spectacle of flood in many vineyards." That's 1885. I'm looking at 1897 now . . .you hear me?

'We hear you,' Dolan had raised his voice.

'1897. I'm quoting. "We had in the April vines a confluence of hail. This occurrence over four days, which together with overnight frost to below our zero of Centigrade, left that hail on the ground in depth to the level of a man's upper boot. These conditions never experienced in this writer's lifetime. Close following this event the weather changed dramatically to fitful sunshine. But the frost had totally lost us the flowering . . ."'

Dolan took it in, couldn't believe for the moment that he'd solved it — his mind racing back and forth, rechecking the combinations, discarding the frost, reconsidering it again, and then dismissing it, homing in on the snow, the hail, not for what they were, but for what they could cause. He said it so sharply to Reuben, it was almost pitched as a shout. 'Get the guy who was here. Aldin . . .'

Reuben took the cue of the voice's urgency. 'Okay,' he scurried off down the truck to the front.

'What's happening?' Leacock wanted to know.

'Hold on a minute. Phylloxera lives in the roots. There was snow. Then there was hail. I think I've got it . . .'

Aldin was back, moving fast down the compartment to grab up the two-way. 'Yes?'

'Listen to this. 1885. Heavy snow. The snow melted and flooded the vineyards. 1897, a crazy phenomenon of hail that stayed on the ground because of frost. It piled up for four days. Then it melted, presumably causing flooding. D'you understand, maybe scientists can clone, engineer phyllox, maybe make strains of them resistant to D.D.T., gas, anything. But they live in the roots. All phylloxera live in the roots. Until flooding comes. D'you get it, Aldin? The buggers can't swim!'

Aldin stood unmoving, expressionless.

'So you push this truck down the beach into the ocean. When it's right under the water, you get a couple of divers to swim down and get me out.'

Aldin was uncertain. 'Wouldn't Markovicz have known this?'

'Look at this situation as it's presented. His was a scientific mind. He was taking a bug and perfecting a strain along the lines he thought other scientists would be working. He wasn't thinking about a problem like — would the fields of our enemies, would the land mass as big as continents, suddenly all be completely flooded . . .'

Aldin had turned towards the two field telephones and Reuben. 'Mr Weiss, Mr Leacock, Mr Weitzelman, d'you agree this hypothesis?'

'They agree, Aldin,' Dolan said sharply over the sound of the voices outside making their various assents.

Aldin made up his mind. 'I'll consult my experts. Mr Weiss, would you leave with me?'

Reuben gave Dolan a small perplexed shrug, then went ahead of Aldin.

'Try not to move about, conserve your oxygen,' Aldin had turned to Dolan.

'Consult your goddam experts. But make it fast.'

Aldin moved his tall stooping frame down the narrow alley and out into the driver's compartment.

Dolan sat down at the table, fought for the moment with the sudden fear of having been left alone. Reuben being there, and even the presence of the cold-eyed Aldin meant human contact. Then he heard tapping, a precise series of small taps along the four walls of the cubicle from outside.

Five minutes passed and Aldin was back. 'There's enough agreement to consider testing your theory. But we can't roll the truck down the beach to submerge it. The sides may cave in as it goes under, releasing the plague in the air. These creatures can float on wind current. This is what we propose to do. Sit down. Listen to me without comment.'

Dolan sat, questioning himself on why he was following the other man's orders.

Aldin raised the walkie-talkie nearer his mouth. 'We're going to get a navy Huey helicopter. The helicopter will lift the truck to a point twenty miles offshore. Navy divers will be waiting at this point. We'll drop this truck from a calculated height into the sea. There'll be a small explosive charge on the outside of the cubicle. As the truck goes under, the left side of the cubicle will be blown in. The divers will get you out. Our calculation is that the truck will still be in one piece twenty feet under water when the charge goes off. There'll be no escape for the phyllox. The only worry then will be to keep you submerged and breathing until your body is cleared of infestation . . .'

'Just hold on a minute.'

'I haven't finished. We're going to set up a TV camera outside, a monitor in here. You'll see everything that's happening to the point of the drop.'

'You can stop there! I asked for Don Hagen. I want somebody to know whether you really plan to drop me and this problem into the ocean, for all time.'

'Detective Hagen can't be got. He's off-watch somewhere. Markovicz may have miscalculated the oxygen supply. These look like one-hour supply scuba diving bottles. I'm telling you categorically we can't replace this oxygen bottle out here. There's a possibility of a blow back, and release of air and phyllox from the inner cubicle. You may not have a lot of time.'

Dolan considered the man's words. 'You know Leon may have got the armoured glass bit wrong, and all his calculations about these bugs.'

'We're positive he got it right.'

'But am I positive he got it right?'

Aldin tried the words patiently. 'What's your decision?'

'D'you know a man called Joseph Stone?' Dolan asked the question gently.

'Yes.'

'Stone would know my decision. You see, he "ran a check". He found I was a "good man". D'you understand what that means?'

Aldin said nothing.

'I'm asking you a question?'

'I don't understand what it means.'

'What he meant, what he said was — it's a difficult time in society for people to be scrupulous. But he felt I was. And I think he's right. So you can drop this truck in the ocean. But make a point of getting me out. Okay?'

Aldin looked thoughtful. Then he gave a nod. He turned and headed out.

He was gone for twelve minutes, timed by Dolan's watch. He came back with three men who acted like acrobats, climbing over and under each other, exchanging sharp instructions, rigging up a battery, power supply and cables, and a monitor, a small Sony TV with no controls. Aldin picked up the walkie-talkie. 'John, listen to me. We're going to have to move the truck again — there are power lines round here, and the Huey's a big 'copter. In a minute you'll have a TV picture from a camera on a slow rotate on the roof. We're going to move you to Orancia Beach, quarter of a mile south. Sit tight.' And Aldin and the three men moved in file out of the cab.

A moment later Dolan felt he truck shudder, as the rearwards tow started. He saw the TV monitor directly outside the glass door flicker to life.

Then came the first views from the camera as it revolved on the roof above him. He was staggered. As the truck, towed by another huge truck, moved backwards up towards the coast highway, everywhere cops and cop cars, soldiers, and military and naval vehicles. In the air at least a dozen helicopters. More helicopters parked along the verge of the road. The direction bleeper in Colville's car following him from Laurel Canyon, must have also signalled the commencement of this major operation. As the two trucks moved down the wide road to the next beach, he tried to estimate the numbers out there. There must be hundreds. The mass of cops and military spoke volumes for Aldin and his experts' estimation of the seriousness of the situation and the danger for Dolan. At the beginning of the journey he saw faces he knew, Reuben arguing with men in civilian suits, Christa standing alone, Colville walking away from her. He spotted Stone with one group of civilians. On the road to the next beach it was all uniforms, no civilians, no one he recognized.

He now realized the camera was capable of being remotely controlled. The panning action stopped as the two trucks arrived on to the hard upper table of the next beach. The camera steadied and took up a position pointing downwards, over the side of the truck, at the surface of tarmacadam and loose sand.

Then the cubicle started to shake. And someone moved the position of the camera to point it upwards and on to the Sony screen came the picture of the descending underbelly of a huge cargo helicopter. And he saw hawsers being winched out, and heard them hit the roof above. And then the camera was repositioned, pointing down again. Aldin, his face even more of a mask, came in and took up the walkie-talkie.

'We're ready for the lift. Go to the right corner of the cubicle. Brace yourself into the corner, get your shoulders wedged under that second shelf, push with your right hand against the upright support in the centre of the rear section. Now the trip to the dropping zone will take four minutes. You will know that the truck has been dropped as soon as the flight vibration stops. You have to stay on the right side of the truck. If you fall across to the left, you'll be injured by the explosive charge. That's it.' Aldin was turning to go.

'Hey, you.'

Aldin halted.

'D'you understand? Markovicz, Colville, you, other scientists, Government. All of you, crazy. But I'm the one in here. I'm like every citizen in the world, the scapegoat for your people's lunacy. D'you understand? This is not of my making. So on behalf of sane mankind, I'd like an apology.'

It seemed to flummox Aldin, and there was a momentary expression of confusion on his face. 'Good luck,' he said flatly into his walkie-talkie. He put the instrument down on a shelf and walked out.

Dolan moved to the right hand corner of the cubicle. He braced himself as Aldin had ordered. He cursed under his breath. He felt lost, abandoned, a jailer in a madhouse, cornered by the inmates, forced to obey the fantasies of their demented minds. The cubicle lurched. He felt his stomach heave. He was in a high-speed lift. This one was rising to hell, not descending. The mirror spun on the table and he caught a quick reflection of himself. He looked like a madman. The truck shook with the huge downblast of the helicopter. The monitor showed the ground below, the crowd, the uniforms, the parked helicopters, the line of police cars ringing the beach, the hundreds of upturned faces, watching his progress. Then that whole picture was sliding idly off to the left. He saw the sea, so near, surface torn to white spray by the helicopter's wind storm. Then the whitecaps were receding as the helicopter climbed, and he lost his sense of place and time, and concentrated on the creaks and cracking noises of the hawsers nestling the truck through the air. He began to count the seconds as he could not angle his watch around. And then there was a moment, the onset of panic as he realized with sureness, with absolute certainty that this was a coffin, that he was to be buried, drowned, with Markovicz' legacy, in a crushed cab a mile below the Pacific.

Suddenly there was a snap, and no vibration, and his eyes were glued on the monitor as the ocean rose to deliver its giant punch. And he was hurled across the cubicle as the truck hit with a muffled explosion. Suddenly there was water smashing straight at him, like a dynamited dam, and a second violent explosion, and he was jack-knifing in pain and choking, and offering no resistance, as his lungs caved in, and he was hurled around and around the collapsing, sinking cubicle. And then the grey sea which was swallowing him changed into the black liquid of unconsciousness.

He tasted the nausea of morphine. In his waking moments he couldn't understand his condition. He felt violently ill the whole time, deeply, unpleasantly sick. He was aware of vomiting, always with a sea of vague faces present, stomach and chest muscles torn by great shooting pains. And yet he was somehow detached from the mess his body was making of its physical existence. His mind floated, gently, on and on, as if suspended like the Markovicz green balls, above a travelator, on a journey to nowhere. And he felt confused, his body going through some sophisticated torture but in the hands of his own mind, detached, relaxed, drugged into caring nothing. In the moments when he felt he was dying, no alarm bells, a sense of welcoming the dark unknown night edging up, coming close, but never quite arriving.

He was in a green cloth-walled cubicle. Sometimes the walls folded slowly in on him, a winding sheet. Other times they were invisible, or just a blur of mist. There were moments when he got the two elements together, the violently wracked body and the sensually floating mind. And then he had sinking periods of worry about detail. He couldn't work out how large the hospital was. One night, through the agony of jack-knifing stomach convulsions when there were six faces around his bed, he judged it a small private place, hidden, secret, perhaps in another country. Another time he heard trolleys banging down what were obviously long corridors and voices receding far in the distance. But then some of the faces in white coats around his bed had distant voices. He could find no scale anywhere to judge what he was experiencing. He gave up. He let them do things, grotesquely foul things like putting wide tubes down his throat and up his anus. And they put him under huge machines on new sheets so cold that he shook so much he couldn't keep his eyelids open.

People talked to him. Stone came in with the tall Aldin. Stone asked his body unanswerable questions. 'Can you hear me? Listen to me. Can you understand me?' The body shook some kind of acknowledgement but his mind refused to put anything into a mouth of bile and burning gases, and acids that locked his teeth together in insupportable pain.

He began to distinguish doctors. They stood over him as if he was the corpse of Julie. They never gave more than a passing glance to his eyes. They spoke only among themselves. They used phrases like, 'Collapsed lung', 'Multiple fracture', and 'Gangrene infection'. The phrases made some sense to him. So he locked them away among the lightweight luggage in some part of his travelling mind. However he felt more sorry for them than for himself. Because he was sure he was dying and decided here were a lot of people just wasting time.

Then a day came and he was aware that he might be recovering. The bastards had found the solution for linking up his broken body with his happily distanced mind. The airplane was descending to make rough contact with the corpse, the solid foundations, the flesh that had housed and owned the escape machine of relaxed thought and unworried logic.

Stone and Aldin now seemed a growing presence. They were there often, sitting at the bedside. They looked in his eyes. Sometimes their looks were wheedling, other times irritated, and their voices were either loud or soft – there seemed no rule for the conduct of questions on different visits.

Then one day the morphine taste had gone, and he knew that something was different because when he woke in the morning the sun hurt him. The bed, still with its cubicle around, still faced the window, but the sun, the same sun he'd basked in for however long, hurt his eyes, even penetrating closed eyelids. And there was no floating now. and when he called out for help, someone to lower the blind, he at last was able to recognize the voice as his own and perfectly coordinated to his thoughts. It was touchdown.

They served him a solid breakfast. He ate part of it.

Stone and Aldin came in as he finished the last sip of coffee.

'Where am I?'

'Hospital, Veterans. San Diego.'

'What day is it?'

'Thursday.'

'What happened to me? What are my injuries?'

'A lot,' Stone said.

'Name a few.'

'Collapsed lung. Several skull fractures, your right arm, six fractures. Eight broken ribs. Four broken – I think it was four, broken – fingers. The main thing was gangrene of the wounds, septicaemia of the blood. You nearly died,' Stone said flatly.

'I know.'

'Very close.'

'And what the fuck d'you want?' Dolan spoke softly, almost in a croak.

'To talk to you.'

'Who is this guy? What does he do in the Army?' Dolan inclined his head towards Aldin.

'Mr Aldin.' Stone turned and deferred to the broadly-built man in the grey suit.

'If you can't understand what I'm saying, we'll come back. Are you able to concentrate?'

'Yes.' Dolan was getting bored, and shaky.

'Then do so. Concentrate on this.' Aldin had a small scar just below his hairline. Dolan concentrated on it. 'There was a project. I'm not a geneticist. Nor are you. So we won't get technical.'

'There's nothing too technical in an explanation,' Stone offered.

'Right.' Aldin was nodding. 'Markovicz started genetically engineering this phylloxera, trying to see if it could produce certain characteristics, and if a hybrid could then be cloned. He was frightened of the potential of an engineered bug in the hands of an enemy. Then he became frightened of the same thing put into our hands.'

'Who's "our"?' Dolan cut in.

'The United States Government,' Aldin said flatly.

'So he suddenly found that it was possible, and then he tried to backtrack – stop all work on the projects?'

'You're right guessing correctly,' Aldin said.

'And you, of the Government, assigned other geneticists to complete his works?'

'To conclude the study to see if it was feasible.'

'And Leon found out, and blew his stack. And you exiled him.'

'"Exiled?"'

'That's the word he used.'

'Okay. Exiled,' Aldin agreed.

'Meanwhile you'd found the project was feasible.'

'We weren't the only ones.' Aldin said it softly.

'Meaning?'

'We negotiated with the Soviet Academy of Sciences and their government, that there must never be a "Silent Soldier". We have agreed a system of monitoring to make sure none of either side's geneticists does work along these lines. May I stress that this is the first concordat ever achieved by us and them, not to pursue research on a technology. And a technology it is. Are you still with me?'

'Nowhere to go,' Dolan said quietly.

'What Markovicz did was obscene. Having achieved his objective, he and his wife needed the support of other scientists in his field, to back up the genetics, and his theory that what could be done by the Defense Establishment, would be done. Very carefully he approached other geneticists. And he approached people of influence, like Hunt.'

'Why Hunt?'

'Hunt was Jewish. Markovicz thought he would get a sympathetic ear for his story about the Defense Establishment acting like Nazis, promoting a "final solution" to the Russian problem. And he wanted funds to complete his work. Hunt dismissed him as a lunatic . . .'

'Was he a lunatic?' Dolan made it a gentle inquiry. 'Was he really a lunatic? Or did he get you people right?'

Aldin began to look angry. 'The bottom line, Mr Dolan . . .'

'Yeah, tell me the bottom line.'

Aldin shrugged off the insolence. 'The bottom line, Mr Dolan, is that if the Soviet Academy of Sciences ever heard that an American scientist had actually produced this piece of technology, the moratorium would be over, and the race would be on. The conclusion, Mr Dolan, has to be that Leon Markovicz was wrong. The "Silent Soldier" will never be made, assembled, engineered by this nation, because we are not mad, entirely mad, as Professor Leon Markovicz was mad.'

'You seem pretty convinced,' Dolan said lightly.

'The plague Markovicz created is at the bottom of the sea. You're alive. You will never talk to anyone about any aspect of this business. This meeting never took place. If you ever try to talk about it, or write about it, we'll deny everything.'

'Who's "we"?' Dolan repeated acidly.

Aldin and Stonc had identical expressions, mixtures of contempt.

'You have fifty thousand dollars in a tin box,' Stone said. 'That's it. If you ever attempt to talk to anybody about what you've seen and heard, have serious fears for your life. To us your existence is not even worth an atom of the sum of this whole . . .'

Daily he got better. They, the doctors, looked pleased, though the huge doses of antihistamines stilled him in bed, softed the idea of *mañana* over the edges of resolution to be up and about and decisive. Three days after the Thursday visit of Stone and Aldin, he started to use the phone. He spoke to the Coroner's Department in San Francisco. They gave him some phone numbers and he finally traced the funeral parlour. Julie had been buried in the small cemetery in Napa five days ago. He shed a silent tear for her. He tried to trace Hagen. Hagen turned up in Idaho, putting L.A.'s case with some evidence in a murder trial. When he did finally get hold of him, the cop was brusque, invited himself to visit the hospital, 'Soon as the shit is over – your ex-wife's butcher friend has been caught. He's for trial. It's all in hand. Tell you when I see you.'

There was no reply from Christa's number. He dialled it two dozen times over the course of the day. He phoned M.I.T., couldn't get through to Colville.

He talked to the Polish lady on the hospital switchboard and asked her to try for Christa Beecham late night, when he would be drugged fast asleep.

Five days after the Stone and Aldin visit, he got a letter. It was a printed card in an envelope advertising a lecture. 'Science and Responsibility', a lecture by Dr Dennis Colville at the Taft Hall, U.C.L.A. It arrived in the morning. The lecture was for that night. Scribbled in pencil on the card was the message, 'Pleased to hear from the docs you're about to leave hospital – they didn't say when exactly. Please come to Dennis's lecture. I'd like to see you. Christa.'

He told the nurses he was going to the lecture. They said he wasn't to. He said he definitely was. Doctors came in and pronounced him fit enough to sit through a Dennis Colville lecture.

Dolan hoped there'd be a question time at the end of the lecture. He had a few questions to ask.

The grey room was not dissimilar in its massiveness and its flat pillars and high windows, to the reception area at the hospital. A bank of wooden seats presented an arched cathedral apse for the worshippers to listen to, and tower closer to the high priest. Colville looked well dressed and efficient. A suit this time, a short collared shirt and club tie, and immaculately polished black shoes. And similarly polished manner.

Dolan arrived late. The bus from San Diego had taken hours – a cab, a half hour to find on the streets near Wilshire, at Beverly Drive. He felt drained, exhausted. His legs were otherwise than some support to hold him from reeling. His arm still cased in plaster, felt like a package of pain. He was short of breath and gasped on the final walk uphill to the Taft Hall, and the wide staircase that greeted him.

There were maybe sixty in Colville's audience. Half of them were sprawled easily – students. The others sat upright, semi-immobile, neutrally dressed – faculty.

Christa was in the second row. There was a space

next to her. He didn't go down to join her, just sat on a back bench.

Colville's voice hesitated mid-sentence as he walked in. Colville looked up at him, then droned on. His arrival noted, but dismissed as of little consequence, the invitation to Dolan, some sop to the girl Colville owned, in the second row.

Dolan tried to concentrate. He felt ill but together – nothing major was about to happen. He was not going to vomit, fart, collapse, or fall into coma. He was just exhausted. And his skin still burned where his clothes tourniqueted across, like at his crutch, or under his armpits. The journey had brought the effect of a week of heavy medication to the foreground. If he'd been fitter, the build up of drugs would be a background irritant. But his body was confused by the action of travelling. Residues of morphine came out from storage tissue to attack the areas of pain and irritation. The trip had started the battle going again. His knees as he sat there, trembled. He cupped his hands round his chin, elbows on the ledge of the back of the bench in front of him, to stop his head lolling and hands trembling.

'The course of man's evolution has been described by Koestler as the pathology of psychopathy,' Colville droned on. 'I see the question in a more fundamental light. I see the identity of psyche as characterized more by the sense of optimism, than the negative view of man, the psychopath. The bedrock definition of genus homo sapiens as separate from all other higher orders, in his abilities towards humour, and that ability to draw, reproduce in lines. I extrapolate humour as source material for optimism. Humour is optimism and is no part of a psychopath's negating. Man is culpably optimistic. The scientist must relate to this . . .'

Dolan watched the auburn hair. It seemed at times to be nodding, very slight movements of approval at the garbage from the stage. He cared, and he didn't care, that the girl was lost to him. If only he could feel indifferent, but he remembered Lake Arrowhead, and the so-called room-mate's apartment. It was another hurt as painful as any in his wracked body.

'After the interval, Professor Weintraub will join me on the podium. We will talk about the specific responsibilities of scientist and his discoveries, in our present culture, and the professor will enrol himself as devil's advocate. During the interval you can hand to him questions which you feel he might ask, elaborate on, or combine into the interrogatives of the issues I've been touching on,' Colville said, and left the stage.

Dolan moved to intercept Christa as she mounted the aisle. He didn't know how to greet her, just looked her in the eyes blandly.

'Hello.' She took his hand. 'When does your plaster come off? There's coffee. I wish I could introduce you to some of these people. But I don't know a single face!'

He went with her, stoned into monosyllables as she asked him how he felt. She finished her few questions with a statement. 'You've been told to keep quiet about it, haven't you?'

He didn't have any answers for her. 'I get to keep the fifty grand as fuck-off money.'

'Fifty grand.' She said it as if she was surprised. But he was sure he'd told her at some point that Stone had delivered the money.

'Yes, you should put in for an honorarium. You and pratt-face Colville.'

'He's been very good to me.'

'He's a fart,' Dolan said flatly. 'When do I get to see you?'

'See me?'
'Why not?'
'Dennis and I are going to M.I.T. You know he's got the post – brand new job, brand new facility. Six million dollars he's got to build a lab for his genetic studies.'
Dolan felt the vomit rise in his throat, but he consciously swallowed coffee hard to push it back and down. 'So that's Dennis's pay-off. I get fifty gees. He gets six million. All because of poor Leon.'
'I think you're being very unfair.'
'I'm too ill to sit through the second part of the lecture. I'll go wait outside in the fresh air. Then, I wonder, would it be possible for you or Dennis to drop me at the bus station later?'
She looked at him kindly, as if she'd achieved some verdict from him that he recognized their relationship was over. 'Of course we'll give you a ride.'
'I'll get fresh air. Where's Colville parked his car?'
'It's about half a mile from here – parking lot opposite the English Department. The second half of the lecture is the longest, Dennis thinks probably an hour and a half . . .'
'See you later.' Dolan walked out through the coffee drinkers and into the night air.

He stood on the steps of Taft Hall. The cold night hit him with a blow that sobered him into another conclusion. He was too ill for the bus ride to San Diego. He staggered across the campus and out into a street, and somewhere found a phone booth and called a cab. Half an hour later it was pulling in beside the tiny house in Venice.
He paid off the cabby, studying out of the corner of his eye, the Chrysler.
The battered Chrysler was parked where he'd

never parked it, nose into the carport at the right side of the house.

The cab drove off. He walked to the Chrysler. So they'd put him in the hospital, then returned his car to his house.

He checked it. He opened the trunk. There, intact, were the two cases of quality Californian wines he'd bought for Colville. He put keys in the ignition and checked the gas. They'd even filled the tank.

And then he knew what he had to do.

He started and headed the car back through the lengthening shadows towards the parking lot opposite the English Department, ten miles away at U.C.L.A.

He got to the parking lot at ten-eighteen. Maybe he was too late. He selected one of the many empty spaces near the main exit. He waited.

He'd been in time.

Fifteen minutes later Colville appeared at a fast walk, didn't see him, walked down the ramp to below.

Dolan restarted the Chrysler, moving it in a semi-circle in reverse, to block the exit. He got out of the car, moved to the trunk, opened it, took out the two crates of wine, tore open the tops of the boxes, pulled out six bottles, hugged them to his chest. He heard Colville's car start up below. He turned to face the up-ramp. A moment later the prow of a black Mercedes nosed round and began to come up the ramp. It stopped mid-ramp as Colville spotted him.

'Here, fucker, here's your wine.' Dolan hurled the first bottle of wine down. It hit the windscreen of the Mercedes, shattering it into a lace of maroon-coloured glass.

'Jesus!' The expletive came from Colville. He tried to open the door of the Mercedes to get out, but the car was too close to the wall of the up-ramp.

The second bottle bulleted down and hit the glass of the half-open door.

'Jesus. Stop it!' Colville was screaming.

'Montelena. Best vintage, '76. But it'd be wasted on you. To enjoy wines like this you need to be civilized.' Dolan hurled another bottle, and another. They smashed on to the hood of the car, sprayed over Colville wrestling to get the engine restarted inside.

"Silent Soldiers", of course there'll be "Silent Soldiers", the whole orientation of science, in the hands of fucks like you, is to violence . . .' Dolan was back at the open wine crates on the floor, grabbing out more bottles.

Colville had got the car engine going, in his panic had not straightened the wheel enough. The Mercedes reversed and slewed high speed into the wall. Dolan hurled two more bottles. One sailed through the broken windscreen and hit Colville's forehead. Colville's upper body reeled back. Stunned for a second, he sat there screaming oaths.

'Ridge Vineyards '76 Cabernet. The best!' Dolan smashed the next bottle on the radiator of the Mercedes. Wine was now pouring down all over the black car.

Colville revved his engine, gauged the opening between the rear end of the Chrysler and the near wall of the exit's opening. His panic calculation was that he had just enough room to get through. He was wrong. The Mercedes crashed into a vice-like grip of Dolan's parked car and exit wall.

Dolan smashed two more bottles down on the roof of the car just above Colville's head.

'You're mad. You're mad!' Colville screamed.

'Never as mad as you. Or corrupt. Dangerously corrupt. Okay, we're all corrupt. I make a living out of it. I'll write up any wines if I'm given a couple of cases. But the difference is, fuck you, I'm no one – you have power, you shitting bastard!'

Now Colville was trying again to get out of the car, but the Chrysler's rear fender was buried in the driver's door.

'Hey, shit scientist. Genius is a risk business.' Dolan smashed another bottle of wine down on the roof. 'But civilization is a risk business. Are you listening to my lecture, you pratt ass?' He smashed another bottle into the rear side window. 'You destroy a Markovicz, we all step back a pace.'

Colville had got the car in reverse. Dolan had moved back to the two cases on the floor, grabbed out more bottles, turned and threw two together. One of them hit Colville on the face. Colville screamed, reversed the car, got the angles right and charged it backwards down the ramp, slewed it into a U-turn, and headed it fast across the parking level below. There was the sound of a crash and the Mercedes engine cutting out. There was silence. Dolan was leaning back now, weak, hopeless, finished. He looked at the bottle of wine in his hand. He opened the passenger door of the Chrysler, reached in, opened the glove compartment. There was a corkscrew in with his driving gloves.

He sat into the passenger seat of the car, uncorked the bottle. He stood up, walked to the edge of the down-ramp. Somewhere below Colville was sitting in the wrecked wine-soaked Mercedes.

'Colville!' Dolan called out.

There was no answer.

'Colville, here's a bet. I bet you fifty grand Leon was right. I bet, what some unknown bastard described to me as Leon's "obscene experiment" will be reality soon – got to be – while people like you breathe air. Colville!' Dolan shouted the name again.

Again silence from below.

'Ridge Valley '78, Cabernet. Good luck with your new six million dollar lab. What you bought it with was another man's life and work. It was all down to him. I'm toasting him for you. To Leon Markovicz, the juggler. To the juggler!'

Dolan drank deep from the bottle. Then he hurled it down the ramp to splinter in a thousand pieces below.

He staggered around the Chrysler, opened the driver's door, and sat in. He sat back a moment and cried silently for his own pain and exhaustion, for the ruined wine, for Colville skulking on the floor below, and for the lost work of Leon Markovicz. He pulled his T-shirt end out from under his belt, wiped his tears, started the car, reversed it around, and drove over the carpet of red wetness and broken glass out into the night.

"A remarkable tour de force".
THE TIMES

DUNN'S CONUNDRUM
STAN LEE

Harry Dunn seemed to have out-spied the masters when he set up the library. Twelve people worked there, and they had access to absolutely everything. All the strategic information, all the secrets big and small – on tape, on film and on paper, they had the lot.

But one of the Librarians had somehow beaten the system, and had clandestinely leaked their biggest secret of all. And with East–West relations reaching countdown level, that left Harry with one hell of a headache . . .

"Tough, funny, quirky, bawdy, suspenseful".
JOHN D. MACDONALD

"The mind-bending fantasy is conducted with earthy relish".
SUNDAY TIMES

0 7221 5485 2 ADVENTURE THRILLER £2.95